W. W. OTEY, The Author

Born: March 14, 1867—Photo: May, 1951

The Tree of Life Lost and Regained

By

W.W. Otey
Winfield, Kansas

Author of

Otey-Briney Debate, Gospel Sermons, Creation or Evolution, The Origin and Destiny of Man, Living Issues, and *Christ or Modernism*

ISBN 1-58427-076-4

Guardian of Truth Foundation
P.O. Box 9670
Bowling Green, Kentucky 42102

PREFACE

Seventy-five years ago, when I was fourteen years old, I read the story of man, and the unfolding of God's Scheme of Redemption. It begins in Genesis first, and ends with the last chapter of Revelation. It was written by men who were guided by the Holy Spirit. In the present volume I have imperfectly retold the story with the hope that others will be led to read it as God dictated it to his scribes. If I could give boys and girls only one sentence of advice, I would say: Read the story of man and his redemption as God had it written in the Bible.

The time was when I did my own typing. As the years leave their work of deterioration on mind and body we need to turn to those who are younger for aid. This I have done in the preparation of this book.

I wrote and re-wrote; typed and re-typed, *The Origin and Destiny of Man*—how many times I do not remember. The manuscript went to the publisher almost letter-perfect. But that was more than twenty years ago. I had to write—or more properly scrawl—this manuscript with pencil. Sister James C. Bays performed the task of deciphering and typing most of it. For this arduous labor, she refused to make any charge. She said, "I want to do it as a labor of love for the Cause of Christ." I do not know of any other typist who could have read the script.

I then sent it to Brother James W. Adams, that he might make necessary corrections. Had I penciled the corrections the typesetter would have been forced to guess at much of it. I deeply appreciate Brother Adams' fine job. When his work was finished, a Sister Craig of Beaumont, Texas typed the whole manuscript again. Her work shows her to be an expert typist. She too, generously refused to accept any compensation for a heavy task.

If this book aids the Cause of Christ in any measure much of the credit must go to these three noble, unselfish Christians, two of whom I have never met. I sincerely appreciate their help in preparing what may be my last book. By the time you have this book in hand I will have likely passed my 90th milestone, but I am making no promise that this will be my last book—I will write more if it be the Lord's will.

W. W. OTEY
P. O. Box 13
Winfield, Kansas

March, 1956

CONTENTS

INTRODUCTION

"The Tree of Life Lost and Regained" is, as the title suggests, a sweeping survey of the history of humanity and the development of God's scheme for its redemption from eternity to eternity. The fortunes of man are traced from the day when Omniscience fashioned a body from the dust of idyllic Eden and "breathed into its nostrils the breath of life, and it became a living soul" through all the subsequent mutations and contingencies of time until man stands in the presence of his Maker, redeemed and transformed into His likeness for everlasting habitation in that city "which hath foundations whose builder and maker is God."

Brother W. W. Otey, now approaching fourscore years and ten (he will be 90, March 14, 1956), is eminently fitted to present such a book to the reading public. More than seventy years of his eventful and laborious life have been spent in the study and preaching of the Book of Books and in the service of the God it reveals. No young man is qualified to write such a treatise on the "Scheme of Redemption." Years of study of the Bible and meditation upon the nature and deeds of humanity plus the experimental knowledge that the passing scenes of life alone impart can qualify an individual to survey God's wondrous plan and write intelligently upon it. Brother Otey's well-known conservatism coupled with the impeccability of his character and his long and varied experience insure both an interesting and profitable treatment of this theme from "the tree of life lost" to "the tree of life regained."

I have read the manuscript of "The Tree of Life Lost and Regained" with interest and pleasure, and hesitate not to pronounce it free from anything injurious to the interests of Divine truth. By this statement, it is not implied that every view of its author on each point is unreservedly accepted. However, even in the few instances in which one might be inclined to dissent from the views of the writer, the wisdom and thought implied in his observations are recognized. Too, no view expressed with which one might have occasion to differ in any sense antagonizes a single vital principle of Bible truth or moral behavior.

One of the most stimulating as well as profitable characteristics of the book is the fact that the personal experience, extended observation, and philosophy of life of its author are interwoven with the pungent comments that are offered on the history of man and the development of God's scheme for his redemption. Not only has Brother Otey preached the "ancient gospel" for more than seventy years, but on December 24, 1955, he and Sister Otey celebrated their seventieth wedding anniversary. His practical observations on love, marriage, and the home emanate from a rich and successful experience in all these realms.

His letters to me in connection with the reading and correction of his manuscript are filled with rich examples of his qualifications to write on such themes. For example, of his beloved, who for a number of years has been "sick nigh unto death," he writes: "Mother's condition is practically unchanged for some months. But of course, she can never be any better. During the last three and a half years of her serious sickness, several times we did not think she could last till morning. During these many days and nights, I have shed more tears than I thought I could. Of these tears, I am unashamed. For 71 years, last night, when we first met, she has been the idol of my heart. How two people who really loved can ever think of breaking up their home is something that I can't even imagine. But so many are shallow in mind and heart." Such passages I have been unable to read without shedding tears over their pathos and tenderness. Brother Otey's book is enriched with many such expressions of the purest and noblest human emotions.

Another noteworthy quality of the book is its homely yet penetrating analyses of the characters of Bible men and women. With Brother Otey and these people of distant lands, centuries past, and foreign cultures, the average reader will weep and laugh. Though milleniums dead, in "The Tree of Life Lost and Regained," they come to life, and though dead, "yet speak." They become as real and interesting as the man across the street or the woman in the corner grocery store.

The author does not attempt an exhaustive treatment of his theme, nor does he aim at a scholarly analysis of its theological and philosophical ramifications. His is a simple, yet pungent, survey of sacred history and doctrine that will appeal to the average Bible student, enrich his character, increase his store of Biblical facts, and inflame his zeal for truth and righteousness.

It has not been my pleasure to meet and to know personally, Brother W. W. Otey. He is known and loved by me "for his work's sake." His life of unswerving fidelity to Christ, the Church, and The Book Divine are a constant source of inspiration to me and to all who know him. I have read with pleasure and profit *"The Origin and Destiny of Man," "Otey-Briney Debate," "Living Issues,"* and *"Christ or Modernism"* —all books by Brother Otey. His writings in the religious journals of the brotherhood I have followed carefully for all the years of my preaching life. These, along with the influence of seventy years of gospel preaching and Christian living plus what is probably his last published work—*"The Tree of Life Lost and Regained"*—he will leave behind as monuments to his fruitful career. It is my considerate judgment that this, his last book, is a fitting climax to his noble service in "the kingdom of God's dear Son." I take pride and pleasure, therefore, in commending it to the reading public and wishing for it an extended circulation.

JAMES W. ADAMS.

February 18, 1956,
Beaumont, Texas

CHAPTER I

CREATION

The story of man begins in Eden, and culminates in man redeemed in God's habitation. The history of God's working in and through man for so long a period is an amazing and glorious unfolding of his wisdom, power, goodness, mercy, and love. Such a story never could have been invented by man. Because it could have originated only in the mind of God, it should be read and studied more diligently and seriously than all other literature. In it, and from no other source, can we learn of our origin and of our value to ourselves and to our Creator. Only in it can we learn the cause of all our sorrows, and the secret of our final destiny. The story was written by men guided by the Holy Spirit. It begins with the first verse of Genesis and ends with the last of Revelation.

In ancient times, men unaided by supernatural power formulated many theories to explain the origin of the earth and of man. These theories are so fantastic that men in modern times regard them as fiction. The story of creation given in the Bible, however, is so simple and sublime, and is in such full agreement with established facts, that it is completely worthy of God as its author. It is safe to say that the Biblical account of creation is in agreement with every established fact of science. Only in the field of unproved theories is there found any disagreement.

The most learned scientists, even those who reject the Bible as a revelation from God, agree with the basic facts set forth in Genesis. They say that at first the earth was enveloped in water; that parts of the earth rose, and the water gathered, and the sea and land were formed. The Bible says, "And God said, Let the water under heaven be gathered together into one place, and let the dry land appear, and it was so." The most generally accepted view of geologists is in perfect agreement with the Genesis account. They teach that vegetation was first to appear on the earth, followed by the animal order, and that man was the last and highest of living things to appear. The Genesis account says, "And God said, Let the earth put forth grass, herbs yielding seed, and fruit-trees bearing fruit after their kind, wherein is the seed thereof upon the earth: and it was so." (Gen. 1 Chapter).

From this it is evident that the earth brought forth vegetation in obedience to God's command. The Genesis account likewise affirms that God commanded every thing in the animal and vegetable kingdoms to bring forth after its kind. There is no known case of this command ever being broken. In every species there is variation but no new species has occured.

At this point in God's creative work, "there was not a man to till the ground." And God said, Let us make man in our image, after our likeness: and let them have dominion over the fish of the sea, and over the birds of the heavens, and over the cattle, and over all the earth, and over every creeping thing that creepeth upon the earth." (Gen. 1 Chapter). God placed man whom he made in the most honorable and glorious position. He not only gave rule over all other created life, but also created him in the image and likeness of his Maker. He placed a greater value upon man than on all other created things. This truth should fill us with a realization of our responsibility, and cause us to seek to glorify God in our lives. We belong to God because he made us in his image, provided our every temporal need, and redeemed us from sin and death by the gift of his Son.

Viewing his own creative work, God said: "It is not good that man should be alone; I will make a help meet for him." So it was that he made Eve as a companion for Adam. Without such a companion, man's life would have been joyless and profitless. Men today, separated from the love, sympathy, and refining influences of women, become coarse and lacking in dignified manhood. Only when man and woman supplement each other, do both attain the highest standard of ethical deportment. The time was, when women were present in social gatherings, that their influence temporarily lifted men to a plane of dignified behavior, but today in many circles of society, their presence does not have the same wholesome effect. In many instances women outdo men in drinking, gambling and other kinds of unbecoming behavior. The descent of woman to man's plane is one of the cancers eating out the moral and spiritual heart of this age. The decline in the high standard of womanhood was perhaps the chief cause of the decay and fall of ancient nations.

The few words of history which follow mark the beginning of the race of mankind on the earth: "And the rib, which Jehovah God had taken from the man, made he a woman, and brought her unto the man. And the man said, This is now bone of my bones, and flesh of my flesh: she shall be called Woman, because she was taken out of Man. Therefore shall a man leave his father and his mother, and shall cleave unto his wife: and they shall be one flesh." (Gen. 2:22-24). The observance or violation of the lessons compressed in these few words has determined the good or ill, the joy or sorrow, of the race of man till now, and will continue so to do while man remains upon the earth.

God stamped upon and implanted in man his own image and likeness, and gave him dominion over all his creation. He gave woman unto man for a wife, to be one flesh with him. What must have been their thoughts and emotions when first they met? In strength of moral purity, and dignity, the earth has never since seen the equal of God's first man except in the person of the God-man, Jesus. The best examples of our noblest men challenge attention and command respect and admiration. Such are held in high esteem as worthy models for the youth of our day. Undoubtedly Adam was the noblest work of God's creation. Surely as Eve looked upon Adam, her heart was stirred to its depths with every feeling of purest love and devotion next to the worship that belongs to God. Who can doubt that the womanly charms of Eve were more enchanting than those of any of her daughters till this day? Even today after sin has left its evil effects, a chaste, pure, modest woman is accorded the highest place of honor and respect, and is held by us to be but little lower than the angels.

There is no record of how Adam and Eve felt toward each other in the relationship of husband and wife into which they were entering. But inasmuch as they must have been—in their ideal state—the most perfectly balanced in body and mind of any two persons who have ever entered into such relationship, their thoughts and feelings must have been deep, pure and exalted. Let us suppose the case of the highest type of young manhood and womanhood today. They devoutly believe in, worship, and serve God. The young man's character is without a taint. The young woman is a virgin without a stain. Their love for each other is deep and of the highest character. Their love is based in part on the fleshly desire to mate and produce children, but theirs is also a love based on that which is far more satisfying and lasting than love motivated only by the desires of the flesh; namely, the love of the soul and spirit. A love based entirely or too much on the desires of the body is not lasting. It is soon dissipated by excessive use and by the decline of bodily vigor. Marriage based on sex alone often ends in divorce. If such a marriage endures into old age, it is lacking in real happiness. In the ideal marriage there is also a union of heart, soul, and spirit, hence a love that is satisfying and enduring and which guarantees perennial joy. Such love survives the greatest trials and grows stronger and deeper as age advances. The proverbial three score and ten, or even more years, serve only to blend the two hearts in contentment, and the purest earthly joy and happiness. Happy indeed are the few who reach the shadows of the evening of life's day with deeper, richer, purer love than in their youth.

"Therefore shall a man leave his father and his mother, and shall cleave unto his wife; *and they shall be one flesh.*" With these words, God solemnized the first marriage. Till this day it is the closest and most sacred union of two lives that pertains to earth and time. The happiness or sorrow of the world depends largely upon its being kept as God ordained. This union should be entered into only after the most serious contemplation of the duties and obligations that it imposes. No thought should ever be entertained that it can be broken by any power but death. The joining in marriage of one man and one woman thus obligating them to live in a state of fidelity to each other till death is God's plan for all of the race till the end of time. Jesus said: "What God has joined together, let not man put asunder." One man and one woman, faithful to each other till death, is God's ideal for man. Jesus grants the innocent party freedom from one who breaks the marriage vows. (Matt. 19: 1-10).

God ordained three institutions. The family, the state, and the church. Neither state nor church can be better or stronger than the family. The decay of the family has been one of the leading causes of the fall of the strongest and greatest of the now extinct nations of history.

The responsibility of husband and wife in rearing a family is greater than many realize. The success or failure of both state and church depends upon the strength or weakness of the character of the boys and girls that they send out to assume the responsibilities of life. Our youth presents us with the opportunity to make the greatest contribution to the future good of the world. Some have lived and died leaving a great wealth of material things. Some have left behind them no material wealth, but have left noble sons and daughters—a legacy of far more value to the advancement of mankind. The problems of the family have multiplied during the last half century. Since World War I, we have experienced a revolution in society. Wives and mothers in large numbers have entered the field of industry. No judgment or criticism is offered here. We state this fact only to show that, for this reason, millions of homes have been disrupted and the task of training a family of children has been made far more difficult.

A generation of sociologists has come out of colleges and universities, saturated with Fruedian philosophy, born in atheistic Vienna, Austria. The first result of this has been that "discipline" is largely banished from the school room. "The natural impulses of youth must not be curbed and natural impulses and passions must not be suppressed," is the poisonous theory. Teachers who desire that the school room shall be a place of civil order and dignity are powerless to stem the tide of rowdyism, and lawlessness reigns. Comic books, radio, television and such like keep children in a state of excitement during much of their waking hours. For parents and teachers to impress any helpful knowledge on their minds, has become a difficult task. How much more difficult it is to get the Word of God to take root in their minds and hearts, with so many things to see and hear! Children from a tender age into the late teens are kept in a constant state of nervous tension and emotional excitement. With such distractions, how are parents going to prepare boys and girls for the future responsibilities and duties of family, church, and state? It is this generation on which the future depends. They must soon take their places in the affairs of family, church, and state. Children cannot be isolated from all contact and association with other children. Such is neither possible nor desirable. This does not mean, however, that no restrictions should be thrown around them. Certainly, they should be protected from such as are known to be of bad character.

The middle teens is a period of crisis. Dance halls, roadside stands, night clubs, where loose morals are in evidence, are more dangerous to the morals of young folks than many can imagine. All too often it is difficult, if not nearly impossible, to prevent girls, even in their early teens, from staying out with boys who are often of questionable morals, and from keeping late hours. And must we be forced to believe that in many cases at the same time the parents are at a canasta party, and imbibing freely alcoholic beverages? I am not optimistic enough to believe this writing will reach many who are so unconcerned about the morals of their children. Yet some parents into whose homes this finds its way may need warning.

WHAT CAN BE DONE?

The strength to overcome evil comes from the heart. Solomon said, "Keep thy heart with all diligence; for out of it are the issues of life." Jesus said, "A good man out of the good treasure of his heart bringeth forth good things, and an evil man out of the evil treasure of his heart evil things." John said, "This is the victory that overcometh the world even our faith." Begin early and take time to teach the child that there is a God, that he is a God of mercy and love, and also a God of justice and judgment. Who will not only reward the good but also punish the wicked. Tell the child of Jesus and his life. Make the story of the creation, sin and fall, and redemption through Christ a living reality. It is the greatest and the most thrilling and interesting story ever told. The parent who truly and deeply believes in God and Jesus and sincerely loves his child can make that story as thrilling and as exciting as the things the child sees and hears every day. Faith in God, Jesus, and the Bible, as God's revelation, can sustain the young and mature even in this generation of trial of hearts. Faith in God gave strength to Abraham, Isaac, Jacob and mny others to live righteously in the midst of wicked and idolatrous people. Faith gave multitudes of Christians the strength to overcome the power of Satan and the enticement of the ancient world. Faith enabled perhaps fifty millions to die the death of martyrdom. Believe me, beloved parent, to plant and nourish faith in the heart of your child is worth more than to leave it millions in money. It is your greatest opportunity to bestow upon your child and future generations the future wealth of heaven. Not only is it your greatest opportunity, but it is also your greatest responsibility. In our present unsettled state of society, it is not an easy task, but it can be done.

The deepest and most lasting impression that is made on the minds and hearts of children is the example of parents. Parents should live the kind of lives that they want their children to live. If parents do not strive to live up to the high standard which they try to teach to their children, their teaching will not be very effective. So to live that their children will respect and love them is the greatest lesson that parents can impress upon their children. At a tender age, children can sense the difference between verbal lessons and an example by living. Even when parents have done their best, if they ever do, some children will go astray. In such cases, some parents have blamed themselves entirely with the failure, and so deeply blamed themselves that they are heart-broken. When children go astray, it is a matter of grief, but parents should not unduly blame themselves. Many cases can be cited of children not living up to the high standard parents set before them. Eli, next to the last of the Judges in Israel, was a very pious man, but his two sons were exceedingly wicked. Saul, the first king of Israel, was a man full of envy and hatred who made a great effort to kill David, the best servant he ever had, but Jonathan, his son, was one of the most pure and lovable characters mentioned in the Bible. David who was a man after God's "own heart" was the father of Absalom, one of the most hypocritical and wicked men mentioned in the Bible.

Solomon was the only one among David's many sons who seemed to have any good traits of character. Solomon started life under the most favorable situation of any of Israel's many kings. He was the wisest man mentioned in history. He married the idolatrous woman from Egypt and built her a mansion. He gathered around him 1,000 women. Considering his opportunity at his start as king, he fell the lowest of any ruler of which I have any knowledge. I think he is mentioned as a man three times in the New Testament. Jesus twice refers to his glory and his wisdom. I do not recall that any inspired writer of the New Testament ever made a direct quotation from him.

Some children are born with bodies that can be developed into great health and strength. Others are born with potentially weak physical bodies. Some children are born with weak mental and moral potentialities. Others are born with strong mental and moral potentialities. The importance of good environment and teaching cannot be over estimated, and never should be neglected. Good environment and teaching should be employed to the fullest extent possible by parents. To provide the best teaching and environment belongs to the parent. Some talents are inherited, hence are determined before birth.

The following excerpt is from the column written by Dorothy Thompson. I commend it to the careful consideration of the reader. I have been saying for a quarter of a century that the trouble of this age is a revolt against restraint. People no longer want to be governed by the laws of man or God. Read it carefully.

"DISEASED SOCIETY CAUSES DELIQUENCY"

"Juvenile crime is a sympton of a diseased society. The fact that it is on the increase in all social classes, and in every kind of community, at a time when the American standard of living is the highest in human history contradicts those who think it can be cured by slum clearance or more playgrounds, desirable as such measures are.

"But slums and poverty are not the causes of juvenile crime. It rages in middle-class suburbs, slumless country towns, and publicly supported housing projects. In hardly a case reported in the press has the crime of a minor been committed because of physical needs. Children steal, but not because they are hungry. They murder, but rarely for money. Many of their acts appear insane—and insanity in all age groups is also on the increase, and—we submit—for the same reason. For the characteristic of all "psychosis" is inability to exercise control —the same incapacity that marks the juvenile delinquent.

"The best modern mental hospitals treat their patients as children in a nursery. The treatment is kind, courteous, but absolutely firm. The patient learns immediately that he must obey; that father (the doctors and nurses) knows best; and that there is not the slightest chance of escaping or circumventing the prescribed routines and disciplines. Only when the patient gets it thru his crazy head that he must be submissive to order and discipline can he begin to get well—which simply means that eventually he may be able to control himself.

"For over a generation we have been progressively rearing children who have never been trained to obey their elders— whether these are parents or teachers. Yet no education, moral or intellectual, is possible except under discipline, involving in the first line deportment, which initially requires obedience. Children are not naturally civilized. They have to be civilized by the exercise of authority, requiring them to do this and to refrain from doing that. But the trend of child training has been against the cultivation of any inhibitions whatsoever. An uninhibited society is a barbarous society; an uninhibited personality is crazy. That is what I mean by associating the increase of juvenile crime with the increase in adult insanity.

"No one who does not love children can train a child. Love, kindness, sympathy, understanding are necessary ingredients of all training. But, conversely, only a saint can love a child who is a self-willed and often savage little tyrant. The downright cruelty of many parents toward their children is often the result of frustrated inability to cope with them because they never mustered the courage to say a firm "no"—and make it stick—when the children were small.

"A child who does not recognize his father's, mother's, or teacher's authority will never recognize any authority, including the authority of the law. The first law is the law of the home. The lawless early environment of the child is the cause of his later delinquency—whether he is brought up in a tenement, a garden villa, or a castle."

CHAPTER II
THE FIRST HOME

God united the first man and woman as husband and wife. He prepared for them a home. He planted a garden eastward in Eden, and in it he caused every tree to grow out of the ground that was pleasant to the sight and good for food. Apparently the tree of life was the most important. Nothing was lacking that was necessary to satisfy their need for food, or to please the sight. It was a garden of "delight." No other husband and wife have ever started married life with everything they needed to make life happy.

They were given the privilege to eat the fruit of every tree except the tree of the knowledge of good and evil. God informed them that if they ate of the fruit of that tree, or even touched it, they would surely die. Our mother Eve seemed not to be satisfied with all that was needed for food and to gratify the sight— the love of the beautiful. Curiosity, the desire to experiment, to try something new, is still characteristic of all people who make progress in material things. Curiosity in spiritual matters that leads away from fellowship with God brings sorrow and death.

SATAN'S TEMPTATIONS

Immediately after the creation of the first pair, Satan made his appearance. He entered the garden in the form of a serpent. All sorrows of the whole human race have come down to us as a result of his coming to the garden of Eden.

When and how did Satan come into being? Many conflicting theories have been advanced in answer to these questions. Some say he was an angel that rebelled against God, most likely Lucifer. So far as I am concerned, I do not know. But I do know that there is a wicked spiritual power among men, and that to yield to its temptation will bring sorrow and death on earth. I know that to resist that power is for the good of people. I know God in his Word called that power Satan, the devil, and other names. I also know that the Holy Spirit by the pen of Peter said, "Be sober, be watchful: your adversary the devil, as

21

a roaring lion, walketh about, seeking whom he may devour: whom withstand steadfast in the faith." (I Peter 5:8). We should diligently heed this warning instead of speculating about where the devil came from. If it had been for man's good to know when and how Satan originated, God would have plainly revealed it. We should always bear in mind that: "The secret things belong unto Jehovah our God; but the things that are revealed belong unto us and to our children for ever, that we may do all the words of this law." (Deut. 29:29). If we give heed to this warning from the Word of God, it will save us from all unprofitable and harmful speculations.

God gave the command not to eat of the forbidden fruit to Adam. Why, then, did Satan tempt Eve? Doubtless he knew she would be easier to influence. To her he said, "Yea, hath God said, Ye shall not eat of any tree of the garden?" Eve replied that they could not eat of the tree of the knowledge of good and evil, nor touch it, lest they die. She knew the command of God, and that the penalty of disobedience was death. Satan admitted that God had said they would die if they ate of that fruit, but set his word against God's word. God said "ye shall die." Satan said, "Ye shall *not* surely die." He set his word in opposition to God's word. Whose word was true? Jesus said: "He was a murderer from the beginning, and standeth not in the truth, because there is no truth in him. When he speaketh a lie, he speaketh of this own: for he is a liar and the father thereof." (John :44). Believe a lie, obey a lie; sorrow and death follow. Believe the truth, obey the truth; joy and life are the reward.

Satan persuaded Eve by partial truth. He said, "Your eyes shall be opened, and ye shall be as God, knowing good and evil." Seeking for "thrills" leads into much evil. Publications are saturated with enticing words, the desire "to know life." It is the Satanic plea that leads countless numbers of teenagers into illicit sexual relationships. It strikes at the very root of all moral and spiritual values. Satan said, "Ye shall know both good and evil." We only "know" in the full sense of the word that which we have experienced of either good or evil. Eve knew good already because she had experienced it in her life. But she did not "know evil" till she had experienced evil in disobeying God. To know good is to be holy and live. To "know evil" brings sorrow and death.

It is my confirmed opinion that we fully know only what we have actually experienced. One can read the definition of faith and repentance, but unless one believes on the Lord so strongly that he *trusts* the Lord with his whole heart, he really does not know what faith means. Mere intellectual assent to the fact that Jesus is the Son of God is not the degree of faith that trusts the Lord in every time of need. True repentance produces in the heart deepest sorrow for sin, and leads to a holy life.

The pitiable victim of bondage to alcohol and to narcotics knows the terrible shame, suffering and sorrow that comes to such unfortunate victims. If we could know their misery and helplessness, we would make greater efforts to help such weak ones to break their chains, and would try harder to prevent thoughtless youth from falling victims to these soul-destroying evils of Satan. Perhaps Satan ruins more boys and girls with alcohol and narcotics than with any other of his devices. It is likely that the majority of teen-agers are enticed into evil by a desire to learn *what it is like.* Curiosity to pry into new experiences leads countless numbers to the ruin of the body and the death of the soul.

Eve "saw that the tree was good for food, and that it was a delight to the eyes, and that the tree was to be desired to make one wise, she took of the fruit thereof, and did eat: and gave also unto her husband with her, and he did eat." (Gen. 3:6). We have our mother Eve's love of the beautiful. More attention, perhaps, is given to make our food "delight the eyes" than to making it nourishing to our bodies. It is estimated that hundreds of millions of dollars, perhaps, more than a billion dollars each year is spent for cosmetics for both men and women simply to "delight the eyes." Of course, this is not wrong within proper limits. If we would examine ourselves with reference to the time and money spent on cosmetics that "delight the eyes," we would be less critical of Eve's eating the forbidden fruit. Satan's appeal was to the appetite, to the love of the beautiful and to the desire to be wise. Temptation appeals to one or all of these desires.

God created Adam. He created Eve as his "help meet,"

but he made Adam the head of the family. Why did not Satan approach him to tempt him? Where was he when Satan was talking to Eve? Answers to these questions are not recorded. But it is plainly stated that Eve ate the forbidden fruit, and gave to Adam and he also ate of it. He knew the command and the penalty. Paul says plainly that Adam was not deceived, but that Eve "was beguiled" or deceived. The record does not state Adam's reasons for eating when he knew the penalty was death. We can only be sure of one thing. He chose death rather than to be separated from his wife's company. Whether or not it was his love for Eve that caused him to choose death with her rather than life without her, is typical of Christ's giving himself for the church, I do not know. On this point, I do not offer an opinion.

The day Adam and Eve disobeyed God was the darkest day of all time. "Sin entered into the world, and death by sin; so death passed unto all men for that all have sinned." (Rom. 5: 12). As a result of sin, the world has been filled with sickness, sorrow and death. A return to the love and fear of God would end the present state of hate, mistrust and the threat of a war that could destroy what is called civilization, and bring peace and a measure of happiness to all mankind. Full trust in God can and does bring peace of soul to every individual in spite of the dark cloud that hangs over the entire world. "And the peace of God, which passeth all understanding, shall guard your hearts and your thoughts in Christ Jesus." (Phil. 4: 7). Such was the assurance Paul gave the Christians in Philippi. It is our privilege to have the same measure of peace today.

God called Adam saying, "Where art thou?" He did not call Eve. Adam was made the responsible head of the family. He was required to give account for his responsibility, but he failed to live up to it. His sons till this day follow his example and shift the responsibility for their deeds unto their wives. Many turn over to their wives most of the responsibility of rearing their children. Many children never get the least teaching in regard to the word of God from their fathers. Those who shirk the God-imposed duty as head of the family will be called to render an account for their stewardship. Too, it is not uncommon for some men to blame their wives for their own failure to live as they should.

When God called Adam to give account as the head of the family he said: "The woman whom thou gavest to be with me, she gave me of the tree, and I did eat." He blamed his wife and by implication he blamed God, note: "Whom thou gavest to be with me." A lame excuse indeed, but we have not been able to frame a better one. We are still imitating Adam. Not often do any of us admit our sin.

Eve said: "The serpent beguiled me." Her excuse is the most plausible one any one has ever offered in an effort to escape the penalty for disobedience.

The first effort of Adam and Eve after their sin was to hide with the hope of escaping punishment. When that failed, they tried to justify themselves by excuses. We have followed in their footsteps. When we commit a wrong, the first effort is to hide it. This is true in relation to civil law. We have many thousands of the most intelligent of our men spending their time and millions of dollars to uncover hidden crime against our laws. Detectives, police and F. B. I. Agents are all engaged night and day uncovering crime and tracking down lawbreakers. The first effort of all lawbreakers is to hide the crime and themselves. When they and their violations are discovered, their next effort to escape punishment is to justify their misdeeds by skillfully framed excuses. Thousands of brilliant lawyers get big fees for helping lawbreakers escape the penalty for their misdeeds. Many succeed in hiding their sins against civil law and escape punshment by skillful excuses. It is not so with God. He is a discerner of every heart and sees every act of all men. We often have more respect for the approval of society than we do for God. When in respected company, we are very careful of our words and acts, but often when in the presence of less respected company, we do and say that which we are ashamed to do and say in the presence of those who have a higher standard of conduct. We often show our fellow men more respect than God. Could we but realize that God sees every act, hears every word, and discerns every thought, then our thoughts, words, and actions would be such as to cause us to reach a much higher plane of Christ-likeness than that on which most of us live. David prayed: "Whither shall I go from thy spirit, or whither shall I flee from thy presence? If I ascend up into heaven, thou art there; If I make my bed in Sheol, behold, thou art there. If I take the wings of the morning, and dwell in the uttermost parts of the sea; even there shall thy hand lead me, and thy right hand shall hold me." (Psalms 139: 7-10).

If we keep before our minds the fact that God discerns our thoughts, hears every word, and sees every act of our lives, it will keep us humble and help us to attain some measure of righteousness. We should care more for what God approves than what our neighbors think.

God said: "Cursed is the ground for thy sake; in toil shalt thou eat of it all the days of thy life—in the sweat of thy face shalt thou eat bread, till thou return unto the ground; for out of it wast thou taken; for dust thou art, and unto dust shalt thou return." Labor, toil, and work are the greatest earthly blessings God has bestowed upon man since his fall. He who is physically and mentally able but does not work at some useful calling does not eat honest bread. Those who are willfully idle are parasites on society. Besides, to labor in some worthy enterprise is to attain to a stature of respectable manhood and womanhood. To be idlers by choice does not have the respect of man or God.

God sent Adam and Eve out of Eden to till the ground from which they were taken. Some Bible readers seem to think that sending them out of the beautiful garden was an act of punishment to avenge their sin. Such readers fail to note the reason God gave for expelling them from the most beautiful and pleasant place earth has ever known. God said, "Lest he put forth his hand, and take of the tree of life, and eat, and live forever—therefore God sent him forth from the garden of Eden, to till the ground from whence he was taken." It was God's first act of mercy after man sinned. Had man eaten of the tree of life as a sinner, he would have become an immortal sinner with no possible way of ever being redeemed. He was sent out and became mortal, hence could be redeemed in Christ. "Blessed are they that do his commandments, that they may have right to the tree of life, and may enter in through the gates into the city." (Rev. 22:14). When man, redeemed in Christ, shall have passed through the judgment into the eternal city of God, he will have right to the tree of life, and there, live forever.

Often it has been said: "What we lost in Adam we gain in Christ." We gain much more in Christ than Adam lost. Adam could be tempted by an appeal to the appetites in his flesh. He was tempted, sinned and fell from his sinless state. When we are raised from the dead, the old bodies of flesh and blood through which temptation comes will be replaced by glorified, incorruptible bodies. No temptation can then reach us. The temptations, pain and tears will have ended and joys will have no end.

The birth of Cain marks the beginning of the human family. What Adam thought about this, the first child to be born, we are not told. But Eve, like all mothers, seemed greatly pleased. She said, "I have gotten a man with the help of Jehovah." This shows that she had a regard for God though he had sent her and her husband out of the garden. Following this, again "she bare his brother Abel." Cain, the first born, was not a God-fearing man, while Abel, the second son, was a man of strong faith in God. Abel was a keeper of flocks, and Cain tilled the soil. It seems that they were to typify the flesh and the spirit. Whether Adam worshipped God and offered sacrifices, the record does not state. Cain brought an offering of the "fruit of the ground." Under the law of Moses, given several thousand years later, such an offering was a thank offering, not a sin offering. Abel brought an animal offering which, under the law, was a sin offering. Paul says that Abel made his offering "by faith." (Heb. 11:4). From this, it is evident that God had revealed to them the kind of offering that would be well pleasing to him, for "faith cometh by hearing and hearing by the word of God." (Rom. 10:17). God always approves us when we obey what he commands in the manner revealed.

The Bible says that God "had respect unto Abel and to his offering: but unto Cain and to his offering he had not respect." In other words, God approved what Abel had done, but he was not pleased with Cain and his offering. Evidently the reason for God's disapproval of Cain and his offering was that he had substituted a vegetable for an animal sacrifice—a sin offering.

In what manner God showed his pleasure with Abel and his offering, we are not told. Likewise, we are not informed as to how he showed his displeasure with Cain and his offering. Some have supposed that each placed his offering on the altar expecting that God would cause fire to consume the wood and offering, without the application of fire by the worshippers.

When Abel's offering was accepted and his rejected, Cain became intensely angry. Angry at God? It seems so. God said to Cain: "If thou doest well, shall it not be lifted up? and if thou doest not well, sin coucheth at the door." (Gen. 4). God approved Abel's offering because he offered the sacrifice that God commanded. Cain's response to God's rejection of his offering was to so hate his brother that he killed him.

A godly life is the severest rebuke to a sinful man. Righteous people have been hated by wicked people from the beginning. The first born son of Adam and Eve murdered the second born son, his own brother. Nothing is said concerning the sorrow of the parents on account of the death of Abel by the wicked hands of Cain.

The first sin was eating the forbidden fruit. This led to the sin of Cain which was perhaps as great a sin as any committed since that time. As punishment for his offense he was driven out to till the ground bearing the mark of his sin. He was to be a fugitive and a wanderer in the earth. Envy moved him to commit murder. Envious people are unhappy and filled with hatred toward those who are better than themselves. Strife between brothers and sisters is one of the keenest griefs to parents. Envy and jealousy is always, perhaps, the cause of most church troubles.

Seth was the third son. Eve certainly thought that Abel was to have been the one through whom God would fulfill his promise to her—"The seed of the woman shall bruise his head." —and thus bring deliverance. When Seth was born she said: "God hath appointed me another seed instead of Abel." She had some knowledge, perhaps more than we think, of the meaning of the promised "seed," which was Christ and the blessings through that seed. Some seventy generations later, Christ was born at the end of the known genealogy. One of the wonders of God's work in preparing redemption in Christ is a complete "family tree" from Adam to Christ recorded in the New Testament. Doubters ask how and by whom the records were kept, since the flood swept everything away. There is just one explanation in regard to the genealogy of Jesus back to Adam. Moses was inspired by the Holy Spirit to write the record. If we accept the fact that Moses, the prophets, and the apostles were inspired by the Holy Spirit, then, we are bound to accept the fact that they were by the Holy Spirit inspired to write the facts that occurred long before written records were kept. If we deny that they were enabled by the Holy Spirit so to write, we deny the inspiration of the whole Bible record. We, likewise, deny thus the Sonship of Christ, and place the religion of Christ on the same level with all pagan religions—it becomes no more than the fallible work of man.

God gave the promise to Abraham that in "thy seed shall all the nations of the earth be blessed." To David, he gave the special promise that Christ should sit on his throne.

CHAPTER III

THREE PATRIARCHS

God's plan, in his work for man's redemption, has been entirely different from what the wisdom of man would have devised. Man has always desired to give free indulgence to his fleshly desires, and to have the preeminence over his fellowman. God's purpose has been only to restrain man from that which brings sorrow in this life, and to guide him in that which is good for him in this life and will fit him for the life to come.

By Isaiah, God said: "For my thoughts are not your thoughts, neither are my ways your ways, saith the Lord. For as the heavens are higher than the earth, so are my ways higher than your ways, and my thoughts than your thoughts." (Isa. 55: 8, 9). The thousands of light years that the starry heavens are above the earth is but an imperfect illustration of the superiority of that which God works over the feeble and fallible plans formulated by man.

God's calling of Abraham to go out of Ur of the Chaldees and his sending him to the land of Canaan mark one of the great events in the preparation for redemption through Christ. God's purpose was to prepare a people, isolated from idolatrous peoples, to preserve a knowledge of the only true God. The wisdom of men would have proposed using the advanced wisdom of the Chaldeans. To select one with a barren wife, and to send him to the practically uninhabited wilds of Canaan was a beginning contrary to all that would have been proposed by men. Yet from that one man and his barren wife sprang a multitude of people, as numerous as the stars of heaven and the sand on the seashore. Abraham, Isaac and Jacob are to be classified among the greatest men of earth. Because of famine, Jacob with his twelve sons and grandchildren, numbering some seventy-two souls, went down to Egypt. Later, they were enslaved. After about 430 years, Moses led them out of Egypt and forty years in the wilderness. Finally, under Joshua, they were led into the land of Canaan into which

Abraham had first been called. To them, God "committed the oracles." To and through the descendants of Abraham, God gave Christ, the gospel, and the church, thus bringing the offer of redemption to the whole world.

As a nation, the children of Abraham rejected Christ. More than nineteen hundred years ago their temple and city were utterly destroyed, and the remnant of their number was scattered to the nations of the world. As a race, they have been persecuted, robbed and killed by the millions. They have fled from nation to nation only to be persecuted wherever they have gone. Few are the nations of history past or present who have not persecuted the Jews. In modern times, they have produced noted philanthropists and statesmen. Some have also contributed much to godless nations of our time. What is their future in the affairs of the world? The answer to that question is known to no one except God himself. Our opinions and speculations on that unrevealed matter can do no one any good. On the other hand, stressing opinions has often unsettled many of the children of God. Let us give heed to the revealed. It and it alone will aid us in doing and being what God wants us to do and be.

The call of Abraham marked one of the high peaks of history. The influence of Abraham is recognized till this day. God said: "Shall I hide from Abraham that thing which I do; seeing that Abraham shall surely become a great and mighty nation, and all the nations of the earth shall be blessed in him? For I have known him, to the end that he may command his children and his household after him, that they may keep the way of the Lord, to do righteousness and justice: to the end that Jehovah may bring upon Abraham that which he hath spoken of him." (Gen. 18). After about three thousand and five hundred years the Jews still bear much of his character. In spite of their being scattered and driven among most of the idolatrous nations of the earth, they have held firmly to faith in the one true God, and have impressed the moral principles of the ten commandments upon the best of the peoples of the earth. Excepting Christ himself, the four men who have stood out above others are Adam, Noah, Abraham, and Moses. Adam was first. Through him sin and death came, and from him all

others have descended. God used Noah as his agent to build
the ark, and to start repeopling the world after the flood. From
Abraham, God matured a people, to whom he "committed the
oracles," and through whom, he sent Christ, the gospel, the
church, and the offer of salvation to all nations, Jew as well as
Gentile. Moses was God's chosen leader, law-giver and mediator, he was a true type of Christ.

When the world became so sinful that it could not be re-
formed, the wisdom of God decreed that it should be destroyed.
God's justice requires that the impenitent must be punished.
His love and mercy cannot admit wicked beings into his habitation.

Perhaps here is as good a place as any to correct an error
that seems to be held by many people. Their idea seems to be
that God is keeping books in which is recorded in one column
the good each person does, and in the opposite column the evil
that he does. They suppose that at the judgment the good and
bad are balanced. If more good is recorded, the individual
enters heaven. If the bad deeds are the greater, he is turned
away. Many times I have heard people say, "I want to do more
good than evil so I will be saved." Doubtless many will be
deceived by accepting this false idea. God will admit into
heaven only those who are prepared for the association of the
angels and the redeemed of earth. A full surrender of the
whole heart in loving obedience to the Lord can alone give
assurance of a person's entering "in through the gates" into
the city of God. If one loves the Lord and worships and serves
him faithfully, he will enjoy association with the heavenly
hosts. If it were possible for one who loves sin and the association of vile characters here to enter heaven, it would be, for
him, the most unhappy place to which he could be assigned.
"Blessed are the pure in heart for they shall see God." "Follow
after holiness without which no man shall see the Lord."
Those who love the Lord will love to do his will. Such characters will be at peace with God. Those who have rebelled
against the gracious offer of God's mercy and pardon could not
be happy in his presence even if it were possible for them to
enter such a state.

Perhaps Abraham was more thoroughly tried than any

other man in history. God commanded him to leave his home and kindred and to go into Canaan, a strange land inhabited by a strange people. Abraham's every fleshly desire and personal interest was against the change. He went out not knowing where he was going. He knew only that God had said to go to a "land that I will tell thee of," and that he would receive as an inheritance by promise. He promised Abraham that his seed should be as numerous as the "stars of heaven, and the sand on the seashore." The number is so great that man cannot compute it. It includes every fleshly descendant of Abraham that has been born till this date, and all that shall be born till the race of Jews is no more. It includes the descendants of Ishmael—likely the Arab race. The promise is, "In thy seed shall all the nations of the earth be blessed." (Gen. 22: 18; Gal. 3:16). Vain indeed is our attempt to grasp the length, breadth, depth and height of the scope of that promise. As stated, it includes every fleshly descendant of both Abraham and Ishmael. But the promise, "in thy seed which is Christ," includes every nation on earth, and every soul redeemed through Christ from Pentecost till he returns to gather the saints of all the earth and all time, and to admit them into the eternal Kingdom. Dear reader, all that you enjoy that is good has come to you in fulfillment of that promise to Abraham. It includes all the redeemed in the eternal Kingdom. To no one else did God make a promise comparable to that made to Abraham.

The first of the two greatest tests of Abraham's faith was based on that promise. Its fulfillment depended upon his having a son. He was nearing one hundred years of age, and Sarah, his wife, nearing ninety years of age. It was beyond the bounds of reason to expect her to bear a son. Yet, unless she did, the promise of temporal and spiritual blessings embracing all the nations of the earth, and including the countless number of the redeemed through Christ, would be no more than empty words. Sarah's faith faltered, and she laughed. But Abraham manifested a strength of faith unequaled, perhaps, by any other man of time. "And being not weak in faith, he considered not his own body now dead, when he was about an hundred years old, neither the deadness of Sarah's womb: He staggered not at the promise of God through unbelief; but was strong in faith, giving glory to God; and being fully persuaded that, what he had promised, he was able also to perform." (Rom. 4: 19, 20, 21).

Christians have a better covenant established on better promises, a better offering for sin, a better mediator, a better, great high priest than Abraham or the Jews had under the law. In spite of all our greater blessings, how faltering is our faith!

"And it came to pass after these things that God did prove Abraham." (Gen. 22:1). At the time of this statement, Isaac had been born, and was perhaps 26 years of age. All of God's promises including the fleshly descendants of both Abraham and Ishmael, and all the redeemed through Christ both on earth and in heaven were centered in him. He must have felt deeply his responsibility to guard Isaac against danger. He looked upon Isaac, not only as a beloved son, but also as the embodiment of all God's promises. From the human point of view, if any harm should befall Isaac, all of God's promises would fail.

God said: "Take now thy son, thine only son, whom thou lovest, even Isaac, and get thee into the land of Moriah; and offer him there for a burnt offering upon one of the mountains which I will tell thee of." (Gen. 22:2). It seems that it was God's purpose to make the trial as great for Abraham as possible. "Take thy son, thine only son, whom thou lovest, even Isaac." Four times emphasis is placed on the dearest object to Abraham's heart.

In our day, religious people offer many reasons for not obeying God's commands as he gave them. They say: "What good can it do?" "It is not essential." From the standpoint of human reason, Abraham could have offered objections. He could have said: "It is wrong to offer human sacrifice." Such was probably practiced in that land. Human reason could have asked: "What will become of your promise of blessing all the nations through my son?" Faith in God who gives the command never asks "what for, and why?" Faith leads to obedience. Faith has ever led to obedience to every command of God for man's good. A lack of faith has led to every act of disobedience and every neglect of duty. Truly, salvation is by

faith, but not by faith only. It must be a faith that acts by love
—a faith that loves to please God for one's own good.

After receiving God's command, Abraham rose early in the
morning, saddled his ass, prepared the wood for the burnt offering, and took two of his young men and Isaac his son. On
the third day, he saw the mountain to which God had directed
him. How Abraham spent the days and nights on the journey,
we are not told. We wonder if he might not have thought,
surely God will recall the command. Perhaps he spent the
nights alone in prayer for strength to offer his son as a burnt
offering. Surely no father ever was under so trying an ordeal.

On reaching the mountain of sacrifice, Abraham told the
young men, "Abide here with the ass, and I and the lad will
go yonder; and we will worship, and come again." He laid the
wood for the burnt offering on the shoulder of Isaac, and took
the fire and knife, and went toward the appointed place. As
they climbed the mountain, Isaac said to his faither, "Behold
the wood and fire, but where is the lamb for the burnt offering?" Abraham had not yet told his son that he himself was
to be the lamb for the burnt offering, so he said, "God will
provide himself the lamb for a burnt offering, my son." So
they went, both of them together. Having reached the summit,
"Abraham built the alar there, laid wood in order, and bound
Isaac his son, and laid him on the altar, upon the wood. And
Abraham stretched forth his hand, and took the knife to slay
his son."

It seems to me that this scene in some respects typifies God's
offering his son for the sins of the world. Isaac was probably
about 26 years old, a strong young man. Abraham was well
past a hundred years old—certainly well past the full strength
of manhood. It would appear that we can only conclude that
Abraham talked with Isaac about the offering, and that Isaac
willingly consented to yield to the command of God. In this
way only could it be a type of Christ yielding to the will of
his Father in being offered as a sacrifire for sin. In any case,
it was a test of the faith of both Abraham and Isaac.

The thoughts that filled the mind and heart of Abraham are
not revealed. We can imagine in a small measure his mental
struggle. His only son whom he deeply loved lay on the wood

arranged on the altar. The fire was at hand to be applied. God's promise to make his fleshly descendants as numerous as the stars of heaven and as the sands of the seashore is embodied in that son. The spiritual promise that in "thy seed (Christ) all the nations of the earth shall be blessed" was also in that son. Human reason would say that if the son was slain every promise would fail. It may well be said that no other man's faith has been so greatly tried. But he faltered not. Paul says he "hoped against hope." He believed that God was able to fulfill his promises even though it should be necessary to raise Isaac from ashes. Is it any wonder that he is called the "father of all them that believe?" Is there a Christian who does not feel humble when meditating upon the weakness of his own faith as compared to that of Abraham?

Having prepared Isaac for the sacrifice, Abraham firmly grasped the knife, raised his hand, and called upon all his strength to make the fatal stroke. "And the angel of the Lord called unto him out of heaven, and said Abraham, Abraham, and he said, Here am I. And he said, Lay not thy hand upon the lad, neither do thou anything unto him: for now I know that thou fearest God, seeing thou hast not withheld thy son, thine only son, from me." (Gen. 22:9-17). Did God know before Abraham placed his son on the altar that he "feared him?" Even to suggest that God did not know is to say that God is not infinite in all matters.

"And the life of Sarah was a hundred and seven and twenty years: these were the years of the life of Sarah. And Sarah died in Kirjatharba (the same is Hebron) in the land of Canaan: and Abraham came to mourn for Sarah and to weep for her." (Gen. 23:1-2). While the offering of Isaac was the greatest test of Abraham's faith, the death of Sarah was his greatest sorrow. For more than one hundred years they had lived as husband and wife, dwelling in tents. Their deep devotion to each other is, perhaps, not exceeded in history. Their love was stronger and holier in their old age than in their younger days. Such is always true when the relation between husband and wife is as God intended that it should be. The writer can speak from experience. The good woman that others refer to as my wife, but whom I affectionately call,

"Mother," has shared my labors, sacrifices, sorrows and joys well into the sixty-ninth year. (As this is being written we observed our 69th anniversary, December 24, 1954). The last twenty-five years have been the sweetest of our pilgrimage. I ask pardon of the reader for this brief personal reference. It is given with the hope that others may be encouraged to make their last years in the relation of husband and wife the happiest.

During all past ages, those who worshipped God buried with much care the bodies of their loved ones. Abraham asked the children of Heth to sell him a place to bury Sarah. They answered him saying: "Hear us, my lord: thou art a prince of God among us: in the choice of our sepulchres bury thy dead; none of us shall withold from thee his sepulchre, but that thou mayest bury thy dead." We think of the Canaanites as a godless people, but it seems there were some exceptions among the children of Heth. They called Abraham a "prince of God." His righteous life had made a deep impression on the people among whom he sojourned. Today, a Christ-like life is the most effective sermon. "Let your light shine," said Jesus, "that others may glorify your Father who is in heaven." They urged Abraham to take one of their sepulchres as a gift, but he refused to accept it without paying its full value. He bought the field of Ephron, in which was the cave to be used as a sepulchre, and the grove of trees that were in the field and that were around the border. There he buried the woman who had been his wife for more than a hundred years. She is one of the noblest women of history. She was mentioned by an inspired apostle as a model for Christian wives. With a heavy heart, her husband, Abraham, turned away from the grave to resume his duties to the living, even as we must do more than three thousand years later.

After Abraham's beloved wife was buried, he turned his attention to his son, Isaac. The hopes of all the fleshly descendants of Abraham, and the spiritual blessings to all nations were centered in Isaac. As was the custom of the time, he must seek a wife for his son. Most of the Canaanites were idolaters. He knew better than many today the evil results of the righteous marrying unbelievers. He called his servant who was in charge of all his wealth and bound him by an oath not to take a wife for Isaac from the Canaanites, but to go to his own close kin for a wife for his son. His servant took ten camels and valuable presents and made the long journey. Lack of space forbids a detailed account of how Rebekah was chosen. She was the daughter of "Bethuel the son of Milcah, the wife of Nahor, Abraham's brother." Laban, whose daughter Jacob married, was her brother. Rebekah was Isaac's cousin.

Jewels were placed on Rebekah and presents were given to the family in accordance with the custom of the country. Doubtless the family had heard about Abraham, his righteousness, power and wealth. The family willingly gave their consent to the marriage. They must have thought Rebekah was making a good match. It is certain that the events of history during more than three thousand years have given ample evidence of the wisdom of the union of Isaac and Rebekah. Their influence is still plainly observed. It was one of the acts of the providence of God in making a race and nation through whom to offer redemption to a lost world. When Rebekah came in sight of the home of Isaac, he was walking in the field at eventide. "And Rebekah lifted up her eyes, and when she saw Isaac, she alighted from the camel." (Gen. 24: 64, 65). With becoming, maidenly modesty, "she took her veil and covered herself." Such was the custom of that country and time. We certainly would not want our girls to return to the custom of hiding their faces behind veils, but it would be a blessing if some maidens would show more modesty than we sometimes observe. Becoming modesty is woman's greatest charm. Isaac brought Rebekah "into his mother's tent." And "he loved her," and "was comforted after his mother's death."

Abraham died at the age of 175 after a long life filled with activities, successes and sorrows. His unsurpassed faith held him true to carrying out God's plans through his descendants. Perhaps no other four men have meant so much to the human race as did Adam, Noah, Abraham, and Moses. Certainly they are the outstanding men in history to this date, and probably will be till the last men on earth. Adam is outstanding because he was the first man, and because by his disobedience death passed upon all men; Noah, because by him God saved one family from which the world was repeopled; Abraham, because his faith in God became a model faith for all men, and because God gave him the promise that in his seed (Christ) all the nations of the earth would be blessed; Moses, because God chose him to lead the Israelites out of bondage, and through him gave the law that was a schoolmaster or tutor to lead the Jew to Christ. What a debt of gratitude is owed to those men! More than twice as much space in the Bible is devoted to Abraham as is devoted to creation, the flood, and about five hundred years after the flood. This fact is marvelous.

Abraham served the purpose for which God had chosen him, and, as do all men, died. Death and burial were matters of deep concern in those days, especially when great men were buried. He "died in a good old age, an old man, and full of years, and was gathered to his people." The next sentence says: "And Isaac and Ishmael his sons buried him in the cave of Machpelah, in the field of Ephron." So closes the life of the man whose faith stands out in bold contrast to that of all other men of earth. Of him, God said: "For I have known him to the end that he may command his children and his household after him, that they may keep the way of the Lord, to do righteousness and justice; to the end that the Lord may bring upon Abraham that which he hath spoken of him." (Gen. 18:19).

It is perhaps good to turn aside from the thread of narrative and make some observations on the three men whose names are more often linked in speaking and writing than any other names in history, Abraham, Isaac and Jacob. It seems that God chose to develop a race of people by the marrying of close relatives. Sarah was Abraham's half-sister. Rebekah was Isaac's first cousin. Leah and Rachel were first cousins to Jacob. Undoubtedly, Abraham and his close kin were the most righteous, God-fearing of all the families of the earth at that time. I think we may conclude that God in his wisdom chose to establish a race of people that would bear the likeness of their three great ancestors, as is plainly observed today.

No other man has ever surpassed Abraham in faith in God and obedience to his commands. No blemish is seen in his character unless it be when he told Abimelech that Sarah was his sister, but failed to tell him that she was also his wife. He was a man of great wealth. His generosity in giving Lot the choice of going to the plain of Jordan where the pasture was abundant, and himself taking to the barren hills, has not been equaled in modern times though we have the glorious light of Christ and the gospel. His generosity is seen also in his intercession with God for the salvation of selfish Lot when Sodom was destroyed. I would that Christians might study his life and learn to follow his example.

Sarah was a deeply pious woman, honoring her husband. Paul points her out as an example that Christian wives should imitate.

Isaac was a devout man, but lacking in the force of character of his illustrious father. He was very partial in favoring his worldly son, Esau.

Rebekah was a woman of great strength of character. She was deeply interested in the future of her favorite son, Jacob. She and Jacob deceived Isaac in order to get Isaac's blessing bestowed on Jacob instead of Esau. Esau sold his birthright to Jacob. This entitled Jacob to receive his father's blessing. The question has often been raised concerning whether Esau had the right to sell his birthright, and lose the blessing. I think Paul makes it plain that it was a fair exchange. He wrote: "Lest there be any fornicator, or profane person, as was Esau, who for one mess of meat sold his own birthright. For ye know that even when he afterward desired to inherit the blessing, he was rejected; for he found no place for a change of mind in his father, though he sought it diligently with tears." (Heb. 12:16, 17). There can be no doubt that it was a fair exchange. However, the deception of Rebekah and Jacob in obtaining the blessing was wrong even as deception is now wrong. It was a case of God's overruling evil for good just as it was in the case of Joseph's brothers' selling him into slavery.

Jacob was a shrewd business man from his youth. His descendants, the Jews, have been noted for their business success till the present. For one mess of pottage he bought the coveted birthright from Esau, but it cost him 20 years

in exile, and more than five hundred head of livestock to pur-
chase peace with his brother so that he might return to his
homeland.

When Joseph presented his father to Pharaoh, he asked him
his age. Jacob replied: "The days of the years of my pilgrimage
are a hundred and thirty years: few and evil have been the
years of my life, and they have not attained unto the days of
the years of the life of my fathers in the days of their pilgrimage." (Gen. 47:9). Truly could Jacob say that "evil had been
the days" of his life. There was much to cause the deepest sor-
sow in his life. Levi and Simeon, his sons, made a solemn
covenant with Hamor and Shechem that they did not intend
to keep. Instead, they killed all of the men of a whole village.
Jacob had to take all his family and flee to avoid being slain.
Because of obtaining the blessing of his father, he had to flee
to his uncle Laban in Padan-aram. By the trickery of Laban,
he had to serve fourteen years for his two wives. He then
served Laban six years on agreement for livestock. Laban
was so unjust in his dealings that he could not endure to remain
under Laban's rule. He had to choose between further in-
justice or returning to Canaan and facing the wrath of his
brother Esau which had been smouldering for twenty years.
If you want to learn how deeply a good and great man can
suffer from fear, read Genesis 32 and 33. Perhaps his deepest
grief was caused by ten of his sons selling their brother, his
favorite son, Joseph. He deeply mourned for Joseph believing that some wild beast had slain him. Only sorrows can
purge the souls of even the righteous. Sorrow keeps them
humble and teaches them that God is their helper and refuge
in time of every storm.

Paul wrote: "And not only so, but we glory in tribulations
also: knowing that tribulation worketh patience; and patience,
experience; and experience, hope; And hope maketh not
ashamed; because the love of God is shed abroad in our hearts
by the Holy Spirit which is given unto us." (Rom. 5:3-5). How
few of us have reached this happy state.

When Isaac was old enough to be weaned, Abraham made a
great feast for the occasion. Ishmael, Abraham's son by Hagar,
the Egyptian woman, "mocked" him. He was about fourteen

years old. This deeply aroused the resentment of Sarah. For the son of a handmaid to make fun of her own son was too much for her to bear. She decided that Hagar and Ishmael must be sent away—that he should not be "heir" with her own son. The great man, Abraham, ruled against his beloved wife, and declared Hagar and Ishmael should stay. Had Abraham and Sarah been left to settle their differences, we know not what might have been the outcome, but God intervened to settle the dispute. He ruled in Sarah's favor. So far as the record tells us, it was the first and only time God reversed Abraham's decision. God's plan for bringing redemption was not centered in Ishmael, but in Isaac, so Hagar and Ishmael were sent away. Sarah's declaration that the son of the bond-woman should not inherit with her son prevailed. This typi-fied the law and the Gospel. (See Gal. 4:21-34).

Ishmael became the father of twelve princes, corresponding to the twelve sons of Jacob. Many believe that the Arabs are the descendants of Ishmael, as the Israelites or Jews are de-scended from Jacob.

There is no record that Isaac and Ishmael ever met after Hagar was sent away because he mocked or made fun of Isaac until they met to bury Abraham. Whether they were friendly as brothers, or whether they were still internally hostile, and outwardly civil because of mutual sorrow while burying their father, we do not and need not know. There is no record of the two brothers meeting again.

Isaac was a pious man, but had far less strength of character than his father Abraham or his son Jacob. His father "gave him all he had" after making gifts to his sons by Keturah. He sent them to the east. He did not want them to live near Isaac.

Isaac was forty years old when he was married, and was sixty years old when the twins were born. The first of the twins was read, or ruddy, and hairy like a garment. He was called Esau, and from him sprang the nation called Edomites. The second son was named Jacob, from whom came all who were called Israelites, or Jews, till this day. As all boys must, they grew to manhood, and chose their occupations. Esau depended upon his skill as a hunter to supply his living. Jacob seemed to desire a more stable source of income. Esau came in one day empty handed. He was hungry and faint. He asked Jacob, "Feed me, I pray thee, with that same red pottage." Jacob showed the kind of "driving a sharp bargain" that is very characteristic of all his descendants down to our time. It seems that Esau had only one thing which Jacob desired, Esau's "birthright." Certainly, that was regarded as being of great value by Jacob. One authority says it was "the rights and privileges of the first born." These were very important—the chiefest being the privilege of serving as the family priest. (Exodus 4:20). Too, they had a double portion of the inheritance. We can imagine how greatly Jacob desired to have the birthright. Esau said, "I am about to die; and what good shall the birthright do me?" He seemed to think that he would die without food. He would rather live without the privileges of the birthright than to die and lose both. Paul warns Christians to exercise care "lest there be any fornicators, or profane person, as Esau, who for one mess of meat sold his own birthright." (Heb. 12:16). The great lesson in this incident is found in the fact that Esau was not willing to endure present sacrifice for future, greater blessings. He warns that Christians should not sell their right to an eternal inheritance for present fleshly satisfaction. "So Esau despised his birthright." (Gen. 25:24-34).

Whether Esau could rightfully sell the privilege that he inherited by birth has been much discussed. Personally, I know of no reason why the bargain could not properly be made by mature men. It may be said that Jacob took advantage of Esau's immediate need for food. It may also be said that Esau had brought on himself his need for food by his own lack of foresight in making provision for the future. It was a deal between two men, for what one certainly valued very highly, and which the other "despised." Like many others, Esau deeply regretted his act when it was too late to change. All good things are attained by labor, foresight and sacrifice of present pleasures for future joys. Present indulgence is the road to future sorrow and ruin.

CHAPTER IV

FAMILY TROUBLES

"Now Isaac loved Esau because he did eat of his venison: and Rebekah loved Jacob." Here we have the record of the first divided family mentioned in the Bible. It led to much sorrow—just as all such family divisions have done down to our time. It all too often happens now that father, mother, and children divide into two groups in homes. Unhappiness always follows. In some cases, when the mother is a Christian and the father is wicked, the mother will gather the children around her, and away from too close attachment to the father, for the moral protection of the children. In the ideal home, as God would have it, Christian parents have deep love for each other and their children. In such families, we find the closest and holiest earthly unity.

The sorrow and evil that follows division in God's family, the Church, cannot be discussed here except to say that strife and division in the Lord's family is the most unhappy of all divisions.

God appeared to Isaac in Beer-Sheeba and confirmed to him all that he had promised to Abraham. "And he builded an altar there, and called upon the name of Jehovah, and pitched his tent there." (Gen. 26:25). He was in the midst of wicked people, but continued to worship and serve God. Strong faith has always enabled men to worship and serve God regardless of trials. Only a weak faith causes Christians to let hold of the Lord, and drift back into a lost state.

Isaac grew old, and could not see. He knew his time was short, so he called Esau and said: "Behold now, I am old, I know not the day of my death. Take your quiver and bow, and go take some vension, and bring some food so that I can bless thee before I die." Jacob had bought his birthright, but the prophetic blessing of Isaac was the matter of chief value. Unless he could secure the blessing of Isaac, the birthright was of little or no value. The strong willed, shrewd Rebekah was determined that her favorite son should have that which he had bought and paid for. She had overheard Isaac telling Esau to bring his favorite dish so that he could bless him. She told Jacob to hurry out to his flock and kill a kid, so that she could prepare it for Jacob to take to his father and obtain the blessing. Jacob hesitated. He said, "Esau is a hairy man and I am a smooth man. My father might feel me, and I might seem to him a deceiver, and he would pronounce upon me a curse instead of a blessing." An intelligent, strong willed woman is about the hardest of all persons to defeat concerning that on which her heart is set.

The kid that doubtless tasted much like deer meat was prepared. Rebekah did not overlook any detail that was needed to convince her blind husband. She took Esau's garments and put them on Jacob. She put the kid's skin on his hands and neck. Thus skillfully disguised, Jacob, evidently with much fear, came into the presence of his father. He told his father that he had prepared his venison, and asked him to eat it and "bless" him. Isaac was suspicious. He asked how he had found his deer and prepared it so soon. Jacob replied: "Because the Lord thy God sent me good speed." This did not satisfy Isaac. He said: "Come near, I pray thee, that I may feel thee, my son, whether thou be my very son Esau or not." We can only imagine how guilty Jacob felt. He knew that if his deception failed, he would likely receive a curse instead of a blessing. Those in our day who perpetrate deceptions and illegal acts live in fear lest they be unmasked and made to suffer their just penalties. Planned deception is always wrong. It robs the deceiver of all feeling of true manhood and self-respect. Rebekah had not overlooked any thing in the details of the deception. Jacob could not refuse to come near his father. To do so would reveal the fraud. Isaac said: "The voice is Jacob's voice, but the hands are the hands of Esau." In the blessing Isaac said: "Be lord over thy brethren, and let thy mother's sons bow down to thee." This was a prophetic blessing, and was fulfilled long years later when the Israelites in Canaan ruled over the Edomites, the descendants of Esau.

As soon as Jacob had gone out, Esau came in and told his father that he had come with the venison and asked for his blessing. The deception of Jacob was soon made plain. "Isaac trembled very exceedingly, and said, who then is he that hath taken venison and brought it to me, and I have eaten of all before thou comest, and have blessed him? Yea, and he shall be blessed." Isaac did not recall the blessing bestowed on Jacob, nor did he give another blessing that would give Esau the preeminence which had been his at the first. (Gen. 27).

The question as to whether Rebekah and Jacob sinned in their deception and false statements has been raised at different times. One man of the highest rank in the Church (whose name I withhold) stated that "where there is no law, there is no transgression," and as this occurred before the law was given by Moses, their falsehood and fraud were not sinful. I am quite sure he was wrong in this. So far as the Bible record shows, God had not told Cain or given a law that it was a sin to kill. God said to Cain: "If thou doest not well, sin coucheth at the door." What "law" had Cain broken? The inherent knowledge of that which is morally right and wrong that God placed in man's heart when he created him in his own "likeness and image" is the law broken by Cain. Paul said: "For when the Gentiles have not the law (of Moses) do by nature the things of the law, these, not having the law (of Moses) are the law unto themselves; in that they show the work of the law written in their hearts, their conscience bearing witness therewith, and their thoughts the meanwhile accusing or else excusing one another." (Romans 2:15). This has reference to the moral principles of the law of Moses, not to the ceremonial observances.

The command to love God did not make it right. It was commanded because it was always right. The command to love thy neighbor as thyself did not make it right, it was right from the creation. The same is true about all other moral commands. The moral law was right from the beginning. Ceremonial commands were right under the law, and are right under the Gospel only because God commanded them. Abraham, Isaac and Jacob were all great and good men, but were not perfect men. God recorded their mistakes as well as their virtues. Had they been described as perfect, it would be the strongest proof that no such men ever lived. The best in our day fall far short of perfection.

Whether Esau could rightly sell his birthright and the blessing which was a part of it, and whether Jacob took advantage of his hunger, are questions which are immaterial. The answers to these questions have nothing to do with man's duty to God.

Esau's wrath was greatly stirred against Jacob, and he planned to kill him. When Rebekah heard of it, she was alarmed and acted at once to save his life. She urged him to flee at once to her brother, Laban, who lived in Haran, and stay till Esau's fury cooled, after which she would send and bring him home. She little understood the anger of Esau, and how long it would be before Esau's wrath cooled. Little did she think that twenty years later, Esau's anger would still be hot against Jacob. Twenty years and a great present from Jacob were required to make it safe for him to return to Canaan.

Little did Rebekah realize that her deception of Isaac would result in such tragic consequences. Her greatest fear was that her son Esau might murder her beloved son, Jacob. If she could have foreseen the trouble that would follow, we wonder if she would have carried out her deceptive plan. Doubtless she was like those who do wrong things now. She did not think of the consequences of her sinful act.

Much has been said about whether Esau could honorably sell his birthright and whether Jacob could righteously take advantage of his immediate need. Whatever our speculative conclusions may be, the fact is that Isaac blessed him by inspiration. He gave Jacob the preeminence over Esau, even to the extent that he should rule over him. This, of course, did not come to pass for perhaps 500 years after Jacob's descendants, the Israelites, came out of Egypt and became a nation and Esau's descendants had become a nation called Edomites. God's providence brought about many things that we may never fully understand. Who can fathom the deep mysteries of his providence today? These questions are all on God's side; our side is to trust and serve him.

Isaac and Rebekah were divided by their partiality toward their sons. What greater sorrow can parents experience than for their children to hate each other? Isaac kept his favorite son, Esau, with him. Rebekah's beloved Jacob fled to a distant country. One might wonder concerning the feelings between husband and wife. It is not in human nature that the tender affection that should be between husband and wife can exist when deep sorrow has come upon them as a result of their own mistakes. When faith in God, and strong love for each other fill the hearts of husband and wife, they can climb the rugged mountain of *Difficulty*, descend into the *Valley of Tears*, and climb out into the *Sunlight of Happiness*.

To prevent possible murder in the family, Jacob had to be sent away. In those days, nothing of importance could be done without the approval of the husband and father. Jacob must not, as Esau did, marry a daughter of the wicked Canaanites. Rebekah obtained the approval of Isaac to send Jacob out of the country. Isaac again blessed Jacob and confirmed to him the promises that God had made to Abraham—to bless the nations through his seed. He assured Jacob that these blessings were now to descend upon him. Thus did the young man leave his parents and home to go into a foreign land. We may imagine that the parting was in sorrow and ears. He was instructed to go to Padan-aram to the home of Rebekah's brother, Laban.

It must have been a lonely trip for the young man—this journey on an unknown path through a wild and at least sparsely inhabited country. The long journey had to be made on foot, and most likely, with a heavy pack of belongings and food on the back, but young Jacob, who was later called Israel, and from whom have descended the innumerable Israelites— Jews, was certainly possessed of great courage and resourcefulness.

"And he lighted upon a certain place and tarried there all night." (Gen. 28:11). The sad and weary young man fixed a stone on which to lay his head and fell asleep. This, from the human standpoint, was a matter of little importance. Yet, the unfolding of God's plan of redemption was centered in this young man with only a stone for a pillow. He was a vital link in the chain of God's providence which began at the fall of man and will end in man's redemption when Paradise is regained. So important was Jacob in God's plan that he revealed himself to Jacob and confirmed to him all the promises that he had made to both Abraham and Isaac. "And, behold Jehovah stood above it and said, I am the God of Abraham thy father, and the God of Isaac! the land whereon thou liest, to thee will I give it, and to thy seed; and thy seed shall be as the dust of the earth, and thou shalt spread abroad to the west, and to the east, and to the north, and to the south; and in thee and in thy seed shall all the families of the earth be blessed." (Gen. 28:13, 14). The promise of the land of Canaan was made to Abraham, Isaac and Jacob. It was possessed by the Israelites after their deliverancee from their bondage in Egypt. The promise, "In thy seed shall all the families of the earth be blessed," was fulfilled in redemption through Christ. (Gal. 3:16-18).

Jacob was deeply impressed by the revelation. It is likely true that he had heard how God appeared to Abraham and then to his father, Isaac. But it seems that young Jacob was greatly surprised that the promises were now given to him also. "Surely Jehovah is in this place; and I knew it not. How dreadful is this place! this is none other than the house of God, and this is the gate of heaven." He seemed to have the idea that God was present only locally. How vastly broader is our knowldge of God as revealed to us in the Bible. The intelligent understand that God's presence is universal—one can be as near to God in Africa as in Palestine. In every place, He sees every act, hears every word, and knows every thought of everyone's heart. Geographical location means nothing in our being near to or distant from God. "Draw nigh to God, and he will draw nigh to you," wrote James. Hagar said, "Thou God seest me." When in respected company we are careful of our acts and words. When in the presence of less respectable company, our words and acts are sometimes not on so high a level. In this way, we respect our associates more than we respect God, or perhaps this is due to the fact that we forget God's universal presence. No other consideration can make us pure and clean in thought, word and deed like the constant realization that God knows our thoughts, hears our words, and sees our every deed.

Jacob had slept with a stone for a pillow. He rose from his hard bed and continued his flight from the wrath of Esau—his long journey to Padan-aram. How he found his way through that sparsely settled country, we are not informed, but he succeeded in finding the home of his Uncle Laban. The story of his meeting Rachel, his cousin, at the well, helping her to water her flock, loving her on first sight, and kissing her and weeping for joy, is one of the most beautiful ever told. It is so sincere, chaste, and free from so many of the faults of stories written today that it will have a wholesome and elevating influence on young folks who read it now. By contrast with suggestive stories of today, I advise our young readers to read it reverently. It is recorded in Genesis, 28th chapter.

Jacob arrived at the well where his Uncle Laban's sheep were to be watered. There he met his cousin Rachel, perhaps in her teens, a shepherdess who came to water her flock. Jacob loved her on sight, and kissed her. Few cases are recorded of a love so deep, pure and lasting as that which Jacob had for Rachel. He volunteered to serve her father seven years in order to have her for his wife. How different from the weak and vacillating emotions that often pass for love in our day. While there are many marriages entered into so lightly that they are severed by divorce in a few months or years, there are still many marriages based on such sincere, deep love that they last half a century and more. Please pardon a personal reference. I cannot refrain from telling you that we, Minnie and I, entered the marriage relation while we were in our teens. It is now approaching seventy years since that happy day, and we are more deeply in love than ever before. I mention this only that others may also be thus richly blessed. The joining of two lives in marriage is the closest, most important of all earthly relations, and should be the purest and most sacred union on earth. Blessed indeed are those who enter the state of husband and wife with unselfish love, and a purpose to "live together after God's ordinance until death do them part."

Laban told Jacob that he should not serve him for naught, and asked, "Tell me what shall thy wages be?" Jacob set his price on his services. "I will serve thee seven years for Rachel thy younger daughter." Jacob served seven years for Rachel; and it "seemed unto him but a few days for the love he had for her." How strange this sounds in the ears of flippant youth today! Yet the same pure, deep, lasting love is greatly needed in our day. I am persuaded that there are still many young men and women who love as deeply as those worthy servants of the Lord. The measure of love is the measure of happiness.

Even though the seven years seemed but a few days to Jacob, they came to an end. Deep indeed was his disappointment and resentment when he discovered the next morning that Laban had defrauded him by substituting the "tender eyed" Leah in the place of the lovely Rachel. I do not recall a more reprehensible act than Laban's fraud. It was a true index to his character. Later in their dealings, Jacob charged him with changing his "wages ten times."

Though sadly disappointed, Jacob did not give up his determination to have the idol of his heart for a wife. He agreed to serve seven years more for Rachel. He faithfully kept his agreement.

At the expiration of the fourteen years, he contracted to continue his service on a basis of sharing the increase of herds and flocks. He soon became very rich in cattle and sheep. But the greed and dishonesty of Laban became such that he decided he would no longer endure it. His situation was unpleasant and dangerous. To remain under the oppressive rule of Laban was unthinkable, but to return to Canaan would bring him face to face with the wrath of Esau. Though twenty years had passed, he had no reason to believe that Esau's anger had cooled. He must choose between the two evils. Doubtless he spent many sleepless hours weighing the matter before reaching a final decision. There is no record that he ever wavered. To decide was to act with Jacob. God commanded him to return to the land of his fathers.

Jacob called a council of his household and laid before them his plan to return to the land of Canaan. Apparently there was unanimous agreement. Laban was away from home attending to shearing his sheep. It was an opportune time to get away. It was three days before Laban knew of the departure. He immediately set out in pursuit with the intention of bringing

Jacob back to continue to serve him. This he evidently intended to do by violence, but God would not permit him to do Jacob harm. God's plan of redemption was centered in Jacob, so Jacob and Laban made a covenant and made a "heap of stones" as witness.

With his fear of Laban behind him, Jacob still had to meet Esau whose wrath had ranked for twenty years. Since God had commanded him to return to Canaan, Jacob undoubtedly believed that God would protect him from harm, but he suffered agony by reason of his fear of Esau.

Jacob was a good man, one chosen of God. Why, then, did God permit him to suffer so intensely so many times on account of the sinfulness of others? I think Peter gives a plain answer. "Wherein ye greatly rejoice, though now for a season, if need be, ye are in temptations: that the trial of your faith being much more precious than that of gold that perisheth, though it be tried with fire, might be found unto praise and honor and glory at the appearing of Jesus Christ." (I Peter 1:6-7). We are given the assurance, however, that we shall not be tempted above that which we are able to bear, but with every temptation there shall be a way of escape. Only when the gold has been refined by fire and the precious stone polished by grinding are they desirable. "Blessed is the man that endureth temptation: for when he is tried he shall receive a crown of life, which the Lord hath promised to them that love him." (James 1:12). Even Jesus himself suffered shame, sorrow, and pain more than anyone else. There is no joy now and no reward hereafter for suffering because of our own wrong doing.

Jacob settled his trouble with Laban and confirmed it with an oath. Thus his fear from behind him was removed. The danger of Esau's wrath that had ranked for twenty years was still before him. He could not turn back, nor could he turn aside and escape. Go forward, he must. To my mind, this strikingly illustrates our voyage on the journey of life. Difficult problems rise before us. He cannot turn to the right or to the left. To turn back in bondage to sin is to lose all. However great our problem appears, it must be met and solved, or the "crown" promised is lost.

Esau appeared in front of Jacob's company with four

hundred men, evidently armed. Jacob was helpless to combat such a host. He, therefore, turned to the only source that could give him help. He sent his entire family over the brook and spent the night in prayer to God and in wrestling with an angel of the Lord. He would not give up till he was blessed. His name was changed to Israel. His descendants have been called the Israelites to this day.

If we Christians would face our problems instead of trying to escape them, and turn to the Lord in prayer for wisdom and guidance, our lives would be more useful and happy.

Jacob knew that he and his servants could not defend themselves against Esau and his four hundred. Undoubtedly most of Esau's company had been recruited from the Canaanites among whom he lived. Jacob said, "I will appease him with the present that goeth before me, after that I will see his face." From his herds and flocks, he made up three companies numbering 540 animals. H gave instruction that a space should be between each of the three groups of animals. When each group meet Esau, he was to be told that it was a present from his brother Jacob who was coming behind. Finally, the dreaded moment for Jacob came. He met Esau face to face. To show his peaceful intentions and his surrender to Esau, he bowed to the earth seven times. Whether it was the gift of 540 animals or Jacob's humbling himself that cooled Esau's anger, we can only guess. We do know that the meeting was very friendly. Esau at first refused the generous presents, but when Jacob so persistently urged him to accept them, he yielded to Jacob's sincere offer. Esau generously offered to leave some of his servants to aid Jacob, but his offer was graciously declined. Esau returned home and left Jacob to travel leisurely to his new home.

On the journey from Beth-el to Ephrath, Rachel, Jacob's beloved wife, gave birth to Benjamin, the last born son of Jacob, and then died. It must have been one of the deepest griefs suffered by this righteous man to whom God had renewed the promises made to Abraham and Isaac. The story of Rachel's burial is related in these few words: "And Rachel died, and was buried in the way to Ephrath (the same is Bethlehem). And Jacob set up a pillar upon her grave; the same is the pillar of Rachel's grave unto this day." (Gen. 35:20). Rachel was buried near Bethlehem where Jesus was born. In order to destroy Jesus, Herod ordered all children in that region, two years old and younger, to be slain. The prophecy of Jeremiah was fulfilled: "A voice was heard in Ramah, weeping and great mourning, Rachel weeping for her children; and she would not be comforted, because they were not." (Matt. 2:16-18).

The loss of the birthright and the prophetic blessing of Isaac was at first despised by Esau, but later, he regarded it of such great importance that Jacob had to flee to a distant country to save his life. After twenty years, he still was so filled with wrath it took a great present and evidently God's providence before Jacob's life was safe. Why was it of such great value?

God had called Abraham to leave his home and relation, and go to Canaan which he promised to Abraham and to his descendants as a home. He promised to multiply his offspring and make them as many in number as the stars of heaven and as the sands of the seashore. He promised further that in Abraham's "seed shall the families of the earth be blessed." This promise was renewed to Isaac and should have been Esau's as Isaac's first born. But, as we have previously related, one day when he was very hungry he sold it to Jacob for "one mess of pottage." After thinking it over, he was so angry that he decided to kill Jacob. There are reasons to conclude that he thought that by killing Jacob all blessings would be his again. How like many now who sell their eternal inheritance for the pleasures of sin.

When Isaac died "Esau and Jacob his sons buried him." Esau seemed to have been reconciled to the loss of the birthright and his father's blessing. He seemed to fully understand that the land of Canaan was Jacob's. He took all his great wealth and moved away and dwelt in Mount Seir. From him came the nation of Edomites. There is no record that the twin brothers ever met again.

CHAPTER V

STORY OF JOSEPH

The story of Joseph, to me, is the greatest story ever told except the story of Jesus. It is the most interesting, thrilling, and inspiring of all inspired stories. I first read it when I was fourteen years old, seventy-four years ago. How many times I have told it to audiences, very imperfectly, I have no idea. I try to tell it in part here with the hope that the telling of it may influence the young to read it as recorded by he Holy Spirit. It is recorded in Genesis 37 to 48.

"Now Israel loved Joseph more than all his children, because he was the son of his old age." (Gen. 27:3). Jacob made Joseph a "coat of many colors." Jacob showed his human weakness in being partial toward Joseph. His mother, Rebekah, had been partial to him. Isaac had been partial to Esau. It caused hatred between the two boys, and deep and lasting sorrow to the whole family. Jacob's partiality for Joseph caused the ten brothers to hate him bitterly. Today, we often see partiality in parents toward their children. Partiality causes much unhappiness in families, schools, and sometimes in the church. To be impartial is one of the hardest things for parents and leaders in the church. God alone is impartial. He is no respector of persons.

It is true that parents often love their last children more ardently than their first children. Grandparents sometimes manifest a tenderer affection than the parents. The explanation is that love, like all good feelings, grows stronger with exercise. A good parent who has loved his children for years has a deeper, stronger, purer love than the young parent. The lesson for us is that the longer we serve and worship God, the more we love the things that fit us for a better home. Too, the longer one loves and practices sin, the stronger grows his bondage to bad habits. Many have deceived themselves by thinking that after a while, "We will turn back to the right way." Such they never do, because the chains of sin have grown so strong they cannot break them. Hence, choose the good and ensue it. It will contribute to good health and happiness, and at last, to a rich reward.

Joseph dreamed that he and his brothers were binding sheaves in the field, and his sheaf stood up and their sheaves bowed down before his sheaf. This indicated to them that at some future time Joseph was to have rule over them. "And his brethren envied him." King Saul envied David, the best servant he ever had, and tried to kill him. Pilate "knew that for envy" the Jews sought to have Jesus crucified. Many are the cases where envy has led to great wrongs. Envy will poison the heart and kill every good emotion of the soul. Envy often causes hatred among children in the home. It makes time-saving politicians of those who should be statesmen. Perhaps there is more envy and jealousy in Hollywood than in any other place in America. We are jealous of those whom we fear may overtake and outstrip us in accumulating material possessions and in gaining the esteem of those whose good opinion we covet. Many a man will sell his "birthright" for a mess of silly applause—even a less reward than Esau received for his birthright.

We envy those who have surpassed us in attaining the things we covet most. Such may be fine clothes, more costly cars, or more expensive houses than we can afford. As strange as it may seem, we may envy others because they have attained a greater measure of moral and spiritual worth. We see this evil often in the church of the Lord. And, saddest of all, it is seen among preachers and writers. This frank admission may surprise many. We preach on the sins of envy and jealousy. But we are prone to regard our work as the proverbial doctor whose prescription is only for the patient—he himself is in perfect health. It has long been my opinion that jealousy and envy have caused as much harm to the cause of Christ as any other sins. These evils were among the apostles while Jesus was still with them. The early church was not free from it. The ambition to have the highest place in the esteem of our brethren, as the "biggest preacher," "the greatest writer," or the "leading editor," whose paper has the "largest circulation," is evident in the church today. When someone offers a word of praise for a preacher or writer, we sometimes say: "Yes, but _____." Let it be said here with strong emphasis that the sins of no one should ever be "hushed up" and condoned, it matters not how high the sinner is thought to stand. I have often heard church members say: "O don't mention it. To do so will 'hurt the church'." When sins are "hushed up," and condoned, we sin. Immoral conduct in preachers and other leading members should be reproved sharply. Let all know that the church must be as clean as it is possible to keep it. Great harm to the name of Christ and the church has been caused by the few unworthy men who pose as preachers of the Gospel.

Let it be said here that no one has ever climbed higher on the ladder of moral and spiritual excellence by pulling someone down to stand on. Worthy heights are attained only by unselfishly helping others to reach higher levels. Rapid progress in the Christian race is made, not by hindering or striving to outrun others in that race, but by taking hold of the weak members, and helping them to hasten their pace.

Jacob's ten older sons went to Shechem to find pasture for their flocks. Jacob called Joseph, then about seventeen years old, and sent him to see how they were. As to why Joseph robed himself in his finest coat, no hint is given. He did not find his brothers in Shechem as he expected. A stranger told him they had gone to Dothan. His brothers saw him coming in the distance. One would suppose they would be concerned to know about the welfare of their father and other members of the family, but the poison of envy had killed all fraternal feelings in their hearts. "And they saw him afar off, and before he came unto them, they conspired against him to slay him. Behold, this dreamer cometh. Come now therefore, and let us slay him, and cast him into one of the pits, and we will say, An evil beast hath devoured him: and we shall see what will become of his dreams." (Gen. 37:18-20). Perhaps the sight of Joseph's beautiful coat intensified their hatred. They stripped off his beautiful coat, and cast him down into a dry pit to starve. "And they sat down to eat bread." It is hard for us to understand how men could be so cruel and heartless toward their own brother.

A company of Ismaelites or Midianites (they were called by both names) came along on their way from Gilead going down to Egypt. Joseph was taken out of the pit by his brothers and sold for "twenty pieces of silver." Jesus was sold for thirty pieces of silver. Doubtless they thought they were rid of Joseph and his prophetic dreams which indicated that he would, at some time in the future, rule over them. But like evil doers till our day, they suffered for their sins. Revenge in word or deed is never "sweet" as many have deceived themselves into believing. The cup of revenge is filled with bitter remorse. They had not considered the fact that they must go home and account to their father for the absence of Joseph.

When men in any age sin against God and their fellowman, only one of two courses can be taken. The right way is to repent of the sin and as far as possible make amends for the wrong. The other course, and the one most often taken, is to commit other sins in an effort to hide the first sin. Joseph's brothers feared Jacob, their father, who was their supreme ruler. Their dread must have been enough to trouble them deeply. Perhaps they thought they had committed the "perfect crime"—that it would not come to light. To conceal their infamous deed, they killed a kid, dipped Joseph's coat in the blood, and sent it to their father. I have often tried to imagine their shame as they made their way home.

We turn now to the anxious father, Jacob. For many years I have had an imaginary picture vividly engraved on my mind. I see a servant announcing to Jacob the approach of a man from the West. I see Jacob, a solidly built man, in the mid-sixties. His head is crowned with graying hair, falling to his shoulders. His beard is heavy, falling upon his chest. I see his ruddy cheeks and piercing grey eyes, the most impressive feature of that unforgettable face. He shades his eyes from the glare of the sun, now low in the west. Deep anxiety is seen on his face. Joseph, his almost idolized young son, has been sent on a perilous mission into an uninhabited country. He tries to discern the coat that he made for his son. Suddenly, deep disappointment replaces hope. It is not Joseph but another one of his sons.

I can see the older son as with bowed head and distress he

comes near to his father saying, "Father, is this Joseph's coat? We found it over near Dothan." With trembling hands Jacob takes the bloody coat, turns it around till he is sure that it is Joseph's coat. The inspired record related that, "He knew it, and said, an evil beast hath devoured him; Joseph is without doubt torn in pieces. And Jacob rent his garments, and put sackcloth upon his loins, and mourned for his son many days." (Gen. 37). Jacob mourned for Joseph more than twenty years believing that an evil beast had devoured him.

Let us now follow Joseph down into Egypt. The story of his experiences in Egypt has no parallel in history. In it, we see God developing and maturing the plan of redemption through Christ. Joseph was brought down to Egypt and sold as a slave to Potiphar, a captain in Pharoah's guard. If any young man ever had reason to give up all hope for the future, he did.

Young men in our day often complain of their hard lot as an excuse for making no effort to better their situation. It is not so much the external difficulties which beset a youth that hold him back from worthy success. It is the lack of noble ideals, ambition, and the will to achieve. It is a desire for present pleasure and ease, and the unwillingness to endure hardness and sacrifice for future good. If one sets before his mind an ideal and refuses to take no for an answer, he. though possessed of ordinary talents, can make a commendable success. There is no sign of Joseph's losing hope. If he must be a slave, he desired to be the best slave in Egypt. He was so efficient that his master made him superintendent of all his house. "And the Lord was with Joseph." This is the secret of all worthy success—God's approval and blessing. Yet, to live right is not a guarantee that one will not be ill-treated. Joseph was tempted in a way that few young men would be strong enough to resist. He gave two reasons for resisting the temptress. He would not betray the trust of his master or sin against God. He said "How then can I do this great wickedness, and sin against God?" (Gen. 39:9). He was falsely accused and cast into the prison with the king's prisoners. If he must be a prisoner, he was determined to be the best prisoner. He gave the work of a prisoner the best of his ability. He was soon given charge of all other prisoners.

Let it be said here that the road to success is not one of ease and worldly pleasure. The road to success is steep and strewn with obstacles. Through a lack of faith, courage, and sacrifice many fall by the wayside. It is meeting and mastering hardships that develop the strength of character needed to fill positions of trust. If any young man ever had ground for lamenting his lack of opportunity, surely Joseph did. Evidently, he decided that, if he must be a slave, he would be the best slave possible.

I have long been convinced that, if a young person will give his job, though a humble one, the best that is in him, he will be trusted and promoted to better jobs. A strong desire to succeed, loyal and faithful service will still be rewarded.

Joseph interpreted the dreams of the king's butler and his cup bearer. He told the cupbearer that in three days he would be restored to his position. Said he, "When it shall be well with thee, show kindness, I pray thee, unto me, and make mention of me unto Pharoah, and bring me out of this house." (Gen. 40:14). For two whole years, the butler did not remember to speak to Pharaoh in Joseph's behalf. He was ungrateful for Joseph's kindness. Ingratitude is a common fault. One should never be ungrateful for a favor.

Pharaoh dreamed two dreams. Both had the same meaning. He was greatly troubled, and called in all his wise men. They could not tell him the meaning of his dreams. Then came the chief butler, and said: "This day I do remember my fault." For two whole years he allowed his ingratitude to keep him from speaking a word in Joseph's favor.

When things go hard with us, we are glad to have others help and encourage us, but when all is well with us, we too often fail to extend the helping hand and to speak the encouraging word to our weak brother or sister in the Lord whose heart is heavy and whose soul is bowed down with a load of care. If we would remember that our burdens are made lighter by helping others carry their burdens along the rugged pathway of life, our lives would be happier.

The butler advised Pharaoh to send down to the prison

and bring out the young Hebrew slave. As amazing as it may seem to us, the great king sent for Joseph. Joseph shaved, changed his raiment, and went in to the king. Pharaoh doubtless received the young man with respect, and told him that he had heard how he could reveal the meaning of dreams. Like all great servants of God, Joseph refused to take the honor to himself. Joseph said: "It is not in me: God will give Pharaoh an answer of peace." Like Daniel the prophet, he gave God the glory of revealing secret things.

Joseph told Pharaoh there would be seven years of abundant harvests, greater than had ever been known in Egypt, and that there would follow seven years of the greatest crop failures and scarcity of food. He warned Pharaoh that there would be very grievous times in all Egypt. "Now therefore let Pharaoh look out a man discreet and wise, and set him over the land of Egypt. Let Pharaoh do this, and let him appoint overseers over the land, and take up the fifth part of the land of Egypt in the seven plenteous years. And let them gather all the food of those good years that come, and lay up grain under the hand of Pharaoh for food in the cities, and let them keep it. And the food shall be for a store to the land against the seven years of famine, which shall be in the land of Egypt, that the land perish not through the famine." (Gen. 41). Pharaoh believed what Joseph told him. He said: "Who is so wise and discreet as Joseph?" He appointed him ruler over all the land of Egypt to gather and store the surplus grain.

That the greatest monarch then living should take a young man about thirty years old, from a foreign land, a slave bound in prison, and place him next to himself in authority, is most astonishing and without an example in all the history of man. Modernists view it from the point of our present government of the world, and label it a myth. To them, it is a legend handed down by ignorant and superstitious savages. If they could but understand that God was preparing a people to whom to commit the "oracles," and to make ready for the coming of Christ, they might not reject the story. It is a very important link in God's scheme of redemption. Viewed in the light of God's great plan, it becomes most credible and necessary in the great drama of human history.

Pharaoh put his signet ring on Joseph's hand, had him ride in the second chariot, and told him that only in the throne would he be greater than Joseph. How would politicians of that day, or of our day, have arranged matters? God does not work as man works. "For my thoughts are not your thoughts, neither are your ways my ways, saith the Lord. For as the heavens are higher than the earth, so are my ways higher than your ways, and my thoughts than your thoughts." (Isa. 55:8-9). How much better the world would be had men learned the great lesson set forth in this statement; till this day people are rejecting the wisdom of God in matters of religion and substituting their ways instead.

"And Joseph was thirty years old when he stood before Pharaoh king of Egypt." He was seventeen years old when his brothers sold him. So he had been in Egypt thirteen years. Eleven years as a slave, and two years in prison.

Seven years of abundant harvests came as God had revealed. Great stores of grain were placed in every city. Soon the people were starving for bread. It was perhaps the worst famine recorded in history. We in America can't understand the terrible hunger for bread. Comparatively few have suffered from actual need for bread. Little do we realize the extent of our temporal blessings and spiritual opportunities. We so often fail to give God thanks.

The people in Egypt cried to Pharaoh for bread. They gave their money, then their land, and, when nothing else was left, sold themselves as slaves.

The famine was sore in Canaan also. Jacob chided his ten sons who were middle-aged men for their lack of enterprise. "Why do you look one upon another? I hear there is grain in Egypt. Go down and buy grain that we may live and not die." He would not send Benjamin lest harm befall him. After Joseph was thought to be dead, he bestowed his love and partiality on Benjamin.

In Egypt, they made known their desire to buy grain. and were brought to the great man who had the rule over all the grain. As was the custom in those days when coming into the presence of great rulers, they bowed down to the ground before the man. Joseph recognized them as his brothers. He remembered how they had brutally stripped off his fine raiment, cast him into a pit, then, had taken him out and sold him to the Midianites. He thought they should be taught a lesson to impress upon them their sin. He accused them of being spies. They vehemently denied that they were spies, and said, "We are true men, all the sons of one man. The youngest is at home with our father, and the other one is not." Like all who are guilty of wrong doing, they did not tell him that they had sold him into slavery many years before.

Joseph said: "By the life of Pharaoh ye shall not go forth from hence, except your youngest brother come hither." He put them in prison for three days. Then he said, "This do, and live: for I fear God." Let one of you be bound in prison. The others take your grain home. When ye come again, bring your youngest brother that you say is with your father. Then, I will know you are telling the truth. "And they said one to another, "We are verily guilty concerning our brother, in that we saw the distress of his soul, when he besought us, and we would not hear." Yes, the tears and pleading of the lad Joseph, when they put him in the pit to die of starvation and when they sold him as a slave, had troubled their consciences these many years. Now, when they are made to suffer, it all comes back with increased force. Nothing is more certain than the fact that "our sins will find us out." One often thinks of the momentary pleasure of sin, but the memory of it will often pierce the soul in future life. Some who are numbered as Christians boast of sinful acts committed while young. But remember this truth: *If a sin is sincerely repented of, it never can be told with boasting.* Its memory brings remorse so long as life lasts. Even if there were no judgment to come, sin is a costly experience in this life. Reuben seems to have been the only one of the ten who had interceded in Joseph's behalf. "Spake I not unto you, saying, Do not sin against the child; and ye would not hear? Therefore also behold his blood is required." Joseph understood all that was said. "He turned himself from them, and wept." He bound Simeon and put him in prison as a hostage till they should return with Benjamin. Joseph gave orders to fill their sacks with grain, and to put each one's money in his sack. On the way home they opened a sack to feed their animals, and found his money in the sack. "Their heart failed them and they turned one to another, saying, What is this that God has done to us?" They arrived home and reported to their father all that had happened to them. The thought of sending Benjamin down to Egypt was more than Jacob seemed able to bear. "Me have ye bereaved of my children: Joseph is not, and Simeon is not, and ye will take Benjamin away: all these things are against me." Reuben made a strong plea for him to send Benjamin down on the next trip, but Jacob said, "My son shall not go down with you." Like other good men have had to do, however, Jacob later had to let his favorite son go down to Egypt. It was a question of yielding to circumstances over which he had no control.

Their food was soon consumed. "Go again," said Jacob, and "buy us a little food." Judah said to his father, "The man solemnly protested unto us, saying, ye shall not see my face, except your brother is with you. If you will not send Benjamin, we will not go, for the man will not see us." Jacob replied, "Why have you dealt so ill with me as to tell the man you had a younger brother?" They explained, "He asked us concerning our kindred, saying, 'Is your father yet alive? and have ye another brother?' Could we know he would say, bring your brother down" For the father and sons, it was a trying situation. Food they must have or perish. To risk sending Benjamin to Egypt was one of the most heartbreaking experiences of Jacob's life—a life already beset with almost unbearable grief. Yet, food they must have. The price to be paid was to send his dearest son. There was a chance that he might be held as a slave. Judah made a moving appeal to his father to commit Benjamin to his care. He pledged his all, and bound himself to bear the blame forever if he failed to bring him back. Jacob said, "If it be so now, do this: take of the choicest fruits of the land in your vessels, and carry down the man a present. A little balm, and a little honey, spices and myrrh, nuts and almonds. And take double money in your hands; and the money that was returned in the mouths of your sacks carry again in your hand; peradventure it was an oversight: Take also your brother, arise, go again unto the man: And God Almighty give you mercy before the man, that he may release unto you your brother and Benjamin. And if I be bereaved of my children, I am bereaved." (Genesis 43). Few cases in history record such a struggle between the heart and necessity. Jacob must risk losing his son or he and all his family must perish with hunger. He had exhausted every effort to find another way out of his trouble. In his choice, we see the rule that governed his life. He submitted it all to the God whom he served. What a lesson for us. After we have done all in our power to master difficulties, we should say from the heart: "Father, grant that which is best, and help me to say, thy will be done."

The sons went down to Egypt again. His servants told Joseph that the men from Canaan had come again. He told his servants to "slay" and prepare for them to eat at his house. When he came in, the sons of Jacob were filled with fear. Surely, they thought, he was seeking an excuse to hold them all as slaves. "Is this the younger brother of which ye spake?" asked Joseph. He looked upon his full brother, Benjamin, whom he had not seen for more than twenty years. His emotions were so deeply stirred that he went into his chamber and wept. Joseph's servants sat his brothers down before him, the firstborn according to his birthright, and the youngest according to his youth. So, Benjamin was placed last. To Benjamin they gave five times as much as to each of the others. Joseph told his servants to put each man's money in his sack, and to put his silver cup in Benjamin's sack.

Their sacks were filled with grain. Their brother, Simeon, was released from prison. As soon as it was light, they started home. Doubtless they were feeling fine. Their brother was out of prison, and Benjamin was going home with them.

It often happens that persons think they have escaped from their wrong doings, only to learn that they must still suffer for their sins. As soon as they were out of the city, they were overtaken by a messenger who accused them of having stolen the great man's silver cup. They vehemently denied that they had stolen the cup. They knew they were not thieves. They voluntarily made a rash vow. They said: "If the cup is found in any sack, the one who has it must die, and the rest of us will be your servants." I have never believed in New Year's vows, or vows at any other time. The Christian solemnly promises God he will always do the best he can. This covers a lifetime and every possible situation. The sacks of the ten oldest brothers were searched and no cup was found. Doubtless they flattered themselves that they were about out of trouble. Benjamin's sack was opened, and there was the cup. So deep was their grief that they rent their clothes, and returned to the city. They came to Joseph's house, and "fell before him on the ground." He remembered, of course, how heartless they had been in selling him into slavery when he was a lad in his teens. For their good, he chided them severely.

"And Judah said, What shall we say unto my lord? What shall we speak? or how shall we clear ourselves? God hath found out the iniquity of thy servants and behold, we are our lord's bond men, both we, and he also in whose hand the cup is found." (Genesis 44). Joseph told them he only wanted Benjamin as a bondservant. The others could go home. Many years before they had seen their grief stricken father when they went home after they had sold Joseph. None of them could bear the thought of going home without Benjamin. Judah related the whole story of how hard it had been to get the consent of his father to let them bring Benjamin with them on the trip. He made a heart-touching appeal for Joseph to keep him and to send Benjamin back to his father. The appeal so moved Joseph that he could no longer make them suffer for their past sin. He cried, "Cause every man to go out from me." He said to his brothers, "I am Joseph. Is my father yet alive? Be not angry with yourselves, that ye sold me hither; for God sent me before you to preserve life. There are yet five years of famine. So then it was not you that sent me hither, but God; and he hath made me a father to Pharaoh, and lord of all his house and ruler over all the land of Egypt. Go back and tell my father all these things, and all my glory in Egypt." (Genesis 45).

By order of Pharaoh, Joseph sent food and raiment to Jacob and all his family. As the caravan drew near, messengers ran on ahead and told Jacob that Joseph was alive and ruler over all Egypt. He protested, and fainted, for he did not believe what they told him. But "when he saw the wagons which

Joseph had sent to carry him to Egypt the spirit of Jacob revived: and Israel said, It is enough; Joseph my son is yet alive: I will go and see him before I die." (Genesis 45). His cup of joy was full, even running over. Thanks and gratitude to God filled his heart. All his deep griefs and sorrows were forgotten when he learned that Joseph was alive, and that he was to go see him in Egypt, and to be near him till the end of his life. Here will end the story of Joseph in this writing. Though the story as I have attempted to unfold it may not have been told with the ability it deserves, my purpose in my effort is a hope that some of those who read it may turn to the story written by one who was guided by the Holy Spirit. The one who writes these lines read the story in God's book nearly 75 years ago. How many times I have read it since I do not know. During all these years, I have regarded the story of Joseph as the greatest story ever told except the story of Jesus. No other story can ever compare with the story of Jesus, the Galilean.

CHAPTER VI

MOSES

The book of Genesis closes with the account of Joseph's death and the embalming of his body. Before he died, he took an oath of his brethren that they would carry his bones with them when they left Egypt. God's promise to Abraham, Isaac, and Jacob to give their descendants the land of Canaan for a home had been handed down from generation to generation. Their fatih that God would at some time make good this promise seemed never to have wavered.

During the life of Joseph, the Jews, as they in later years came to be known, were in high favor with the king of Egypt. They were located in the land of Goshen, the most desirable place for their herds and flocks in all of Egypt.

The book of Exodus opens on a different scene. Another king had come to the throne who "knew not Joseph." The whole race of Jews had been enslaved. They were made to endure the burdens laid on them by cruel taskmasters. But the more they were burdened with bitter servitude, the more they increased in number. The king became alarmed lest the Jews should become greater in number and stronger than the Egyptians and rebel against their masters and gain their freedom. With the aim to prevent their increase in numbers, the king commanded that every male child should be killed by the mid-wives at their birth. How many may have been killed, we are not informed.

Under these distressing circumstances, the Bible says: "And there went a man of the house of Levi, and took to wife a daughter of Levi." (Ex. 2:1). Viewing from the stand point of human affairs, this was a very ordinary marriage, but in God's plan of redemption, it marks one of the high points in the history of man. To this union, Moses was born. When his mother saw that he "was a goodly child," she hid him three months to prevent the king's executioners from destroying him. When she could no longer hide him, she made a decision that

68

no one except a mother can appreciate. Only a mother can have any idea of how much it grieved her heart. She made a little ark, like a boat, put her baby in it and laid it "among the flags by the river brink." She put her daughter, Miriam, about thirteen years old, to stand off at a distance to see what would happen to the babe. How marvelous are the ways of God in his providence to bring about what he plans! "How unsearchable are his judgments and his ways past finding out." (Rom. 11:33). The daughter of Pharaoh, a royal princess, came down to the river to bathe. She saw the little ark, and sent her maid to fetch it to her. Doubtless with some curiosity to know what was in it, she opened the ark and saw that it contained a little baby. "And, behold, the babe wept." The crystal tear on that baby's cheek touched the mother love of the proud princess and changed the course of the world. Perhaps no other baby's tears have ever had such far reaching influence on so many people. It extends even to our time, and will continue until time shall end. Moses was saved to lead the Israelites out of bondage and through forty years' wandering in the wilderness. Through him God gave the law that was to last to Christ.

The princess saved the baby in disobedience to the king's command, and as surprising as it may seem to us, she took him home to the palace and adopted him as her son. We might ask many questions about this action for which no answer can be found. Did the king know that the baby was born to slave parents? Why did he allow the slave child to grow up in the royal family until he was forty years of age? Why did he allow this slave to be educated in all the wisdom that could be given by royal teachers? For my part, I can only say that it was the working of God's providence in order to bring redemption to a sinful world.

How he retained faith in God while living among idolaters, we are not informed. Unless he had some contact with his people, we do not understand how he knew that God had promised the land of Canaan as a home to the descendants of Abraham, Isaac, and Jacob. He seemed to know of this promise when he made the first recorded visit to his kinsmen. When he was about forty years old, he chose to cast his lot with his brethren who were cruelly mistreated by their taskmasters.

To leave the royal court with its riches and pleasures and take his place under cruel masters was a greater sacrifice than we can understand. The writer of the book of Hebrews says: "By faith Moses, when he was grown up, refused to be called the son of Pharaoh's daughter; choosing rather to share ill treatment with the people of God, than to enjoy the pleasures of sin for a season: accounting the reproach of Christ greater riches than the treasure of Egypt: for he looked unto the recompence of reward." (Heb. 11:24-26). While we of today do not sacrifice so much riches and social glory as Moses did, the same principle prevails now as then. The pleasures of sin must be given up in order to attain the greater riches that await those who love and serve the Lord. We are promised an inheritance, incorruptible and that fadeth not away, reserved in heaven for God's children.

When Moses was about forty years old, he went out to see how his brethren in slavery were faring. He found they were being cruelly mistreated by their taskmasters. Few men having all the pleasures of a king's court would be concerned about their poor relatives even if they were free. Moses stands out from other men under whatever situation we observe him. He "saw an Egyptian smiting a Hebrew." His deep sense of justice was so aroused that he became indignant. He looked to see if any one was watching, then slew the Egyptian and covered him up in the sand. He went again the next day and saw two of his own brethren fighting. He chided them. As is always true, the one who was in the wrong resented his reproof and said: "Who made you a prince and a judge over us? Thinkest thou to kill me, as thou killest the Egyptian?" Pharaoh heard of Moses' act and sought to kill him, but he fled to the land of Midian, "and sat down at a well." In that desert country, a well was the surest place to meet people. The seven daughters of the priest of Midian came to water their flocks. Other shepherds were accustomed to watering their flocks from the same well. They also came to water at the same time. They were so destitute of character that they drove the young women and their flocks away, and watered their own flocks. Here again the high character of Moses is displayed. He stood up and drove the unmanly shepherds away and let the women have the water that they had drawn. Whenever or wherever we see men of character, whether young or old, we find them defending the rights of womanhood. For men or boys to show disrespect to the daughters of Eve is to reveal one of the lowest traits of character. (Here a whole chapter ought to be written, but want of space forbids).

Moses married one of the daughters of Reuel, the priest, and was "content to dwell with the man" about forty years as his shepherd. Why God in his providence ruled that Moses should serve in that humble work in a desert country, we are not informed. We can only suppose that he needed to spend many weary nights in meditation in order to mature and develop a strength of character for a work which, we can safely say, was the greatest work ever performed by any one except Christ himself.

As a deliverer from Egyptian bondage, as a leader, as a law giver, as a meditator, and as priest—Moses was a perfect type of Christ and his work of redemption.

Moses "led the flock to the back of the wilderness, and came to the mount of God, unto Horeb." (Ex. 3:1). Mount Horeb was where God revealed the law to Moses. Here he saw a bush as a flame of fire, and decided that he would find out why it was not consumed. As he drew near, the angel of God spoke to him saying: "Draw not nigh hither: put off thy shoes from thy feet, for the place whereon thou standest is holy ground." God told Moses that he was sending him back to Egypt to deliver the Israelites from bondage and to lead them to Canaan, the land of promise. What a surprise this must have been to Moses. He was only one man with no army to war against the great Egyptian nation. More still, he had been a fugitive from the king's wrath for forty years. Little wonder it is that he offered every kind of excuse to escape the seemingly impossible task God asked him to perform. We know of no other task laid on any man that appeared so impossible to perform. God assured him that he would be with him and enable him to accomplish the great work.

We would like to follow Moses back to Egypt, talk about the wonders he performed, and tell how the Israelites crossed the Red Sea and entered the wilderness. We would also like to talk about Moses' going up into the mount to receive the law, the building of the tabernacle, the order of worship, the wanderings of the Israelites in the wilderness forty years until all who were twenty years and older at the time they left Egypt died except Joshua and Caleb, and how they crossed the river Jordan and entered the land promised to Abraham, Isaac, Jacob, and their descendants for a home. Much more of Israel's history is interesting and important, but space forbids that we discuss it. We must close here. Next we will talk about Jesus the Christ and his work while on earth.

CHAPTER VII

CHRIST IN PROPHECY

A study of Christ as he is presented by the prophets, especially from David onward, is interesting and edifying to Christians. A whole book would not exhaust the subject. Only a few paragraphs can be given here.

The leaders of the Jews misinterpreted the prophecies pointing to Christ. They failed to understand their spiritual meaning. The eyes of their understanding were blinded by their desire for material things— prestige, power and the desire to rule over others—so that they failed to see him as the Son of man's Savior from sin.

Isaiah prophesied: "For unto us a child is born, unto us a son is given; and the government shall be upon his shoulder; and his name shall be called Wonderful, Counsellor, Mighty God, Everlasting Father, Prince of Peace. Of the increase of his government and of peace there shall be no end, upon the throne of David, and upon his kingdom, to establish it, and to uphold it with justice and with righteousness from henceforth even forever. The zeal of the Lord of hosts will perform this." (Isa. 9: 6, 7).

Zechariah prophesied: "And he shall speak peace unto the nations: and his dominion shall be from sea to sea, and from the rivers to the ends of the earth." (Zech. 9: 10). The dignity, power, and glory of the king who was to sit on David's throne and whose rule was to extend to the whole earth was far greater in extent than that of either David or Solomon. From these and other such prophecies, the leaders of the Jews concluded that the coming king was to be a great earthly ruler, far greater in power and glory than any other king before him. They seemed not to have considered the prophecies that revealed him in a spiritual light. Material riches, worldly pleasure, positions of power, rule over others—these were the things for which they sighed, and to the coming king, their Messiah, they looked for such. Many professed followers of the meek and lowly Nazarene, we are sad to say, have their affections set on the same kind of fleeting, unsatisfying, earthly attractions. The Jews seemed never to have considered what Isaiah said of Christ in regard to a spiritual reign.

"Who hath believed our message? and to whom hath the arm of the Lord been revealed? For he shall grow up before him as a tender plant, and as a root out of dry ground: he hath no form nor comeliness; and when we shall see him, there is no beauty that we should desire him. He was despised, and rejected of men; a man of sorrow, and acquainted with grief: and as one from whom men hid their faces he was despised; and we esteem him not. Surely he hath borne our griefs and carried our sorrows; yet we did esteem him stricken, smitten of God. But he was wounded for our transgressions; the chastisement of our peace was laid upon him, and with his stripes we are healed. All we like sheep have gone astray; we have turned every one to his own way; and the Lord hath laid on him the iniquity of us all."

"He was oppressed, yet when afflicted he opened not his mouth; as a lamb that is led to the slaughter, and as a sheep that is before its shearer is dumb, so he openeth not his mouth. By oppression and judgment he was taken away; and as for his generation, who among them considered that he was cut off out of the land of the living for the transgressions of my people to whom the stroke was due? And they made his grave with the wicked, and with a rich man in his death; although he had done no violence, neither was deceit found in his mouth."

"Yet it pleased the Lord to bruise him; he hath put him to grief; when thou shalt make his soul an offering for sin, he shall see his seed, he shall prolong his days, and the pleasure of the Lord shall prosper in his hand." (Isa. 53: 1-10).

The Jews did not want a king to "sit on David's throne" like the king Isaiah here so vividly describes. They did not want one that was "despised and rejected of men, a man of sorrow and acquainted with grief," a king "wounded for their transgressions," one so meek that he could be "oppressed, yet not open his mouth," and who could be "led as a lamb to the slaughter." Not a single trait of character that Isaiah attributes to the coming king had the least appeal to the self-righteous, arrogant leaders of the Jews. They were looking for a king with an army who would defeat and drive from their land the mighty Roman legions. Still more, they expected their coming king to conquer the Gentile nations "from sea to sea and from the rivers to the ends of the earth."

Christians who live under a better covenant, established on better promises, have not reached a much higher plane of things spiritually. With most, it is a mad race for power, wealth, and worldly pleasures. Should Jesus personally visit religious assemblies, would he be less severe in his rebukes than he was when he came to the Jews who had fallen so far below the ideal set forth in the law which came from Mount Sinai? Are the churches of professed Christians now better than the seven churches of Asia were when Jesus instructed John to write them? I have often wondered if we, who claim we are churches of Christ, could not find a picture of ourselves in the letter to the church of Laodicea. He said to that church, "I know thy works, that thou art neither cold nor hot: I would that thou wert cold or hot. So because thou art lukewarm, I will spue thee out of my mouth. Because thou sayest, I am rich, and have gotten riches, and have need of nothing; and knowest not that thou art the wretched one and miserable and poor and blind and naked: I counsel thee to buy of me gold refined by fire, that thou mayest become rich; and white garments, that thou mayest clothe thyself, and that the shame of thy nakedness be not made manifest; and eyesalve to annoint thine eyes, that thou mayest see." (Rev. 3:14-18). We boast that we oppose human creeds and oppose denominational practices. We glory in the fact that the Bible is our only rule of faith and practice. We can quote with pride Mark 16:16, and Acts 2:3, but we seem to have forgotten the sermon on the mount, the necessity of doing good to them that wrong us, and praying for those who mistreat us. Do we even think of living by the *Golden Rule,* or of the fact that only the pure in heart shall see God? Is it not well that we see ourselves as the Lord sees us? How many of us have "crucified the flesh" and "put off the old man, and put on the new man" in the likeness of Christ? "And now, my little children, abide in him; that, if he shall be manifested, we may have boldness, and not be ashamed before him at his coming." (I John 2:28).

CHAPTER VIII

THE SINLESSNESS OF JESUS

When the Pharisees were gathered together, Jesus asked them, saying, "What think ye of Christ? whose son is he?" (Matt. 22:41-42). The hope of a sorrowing world depends upon the correct answer to this question. If he is only the son of man, all hope of a future and better life is vain. If he is the Son of God, man's greatest hope is made sure. That he is the Son of God may be proved from any one of several viewpoints. The viewpoint to be considered in this chapter is: Did he live a sinless life?

To determine the guilt or innocence of a man there must be, first, a law by which to measure his deeds. Second, true witness. If no reliable witness testifies that the one on trial has violated the law, he is adjudged innocent. Jesus must be tried by the same rule. Too, in proving him to be sinless, it is permissible to introduce certain other evidences that are, in the very nature of the case, not applicable to any other life.

The first incontestable evidence that Jesus must of necessity be sinless is the fact that, in being reconciled to God, man requires a sinless mediator. Sin so separated man from his Maker that he could no longer appear in the immediate presence of God, hence he needed one who was sinless to appear in his behalf. Nor is a sinless mediator all that man needed. A sacrifice and offering for sin, an atonement, was needed that could "take away sin." Such a sacrifice must be sinless, voluntarily offered, and of such merit as to atone for sin. All these requirements are united in Jesus. Not one of them has ever been found in any other one who has lived among men, nor has any so claimed. Jesus came from God. He is as divine as God, yet as human as man. He is the only one in all history of whom it has ever been claimed that he came from God; is as divine as God, yet as human as man; lived sinlessly; voluntarily offered himself as a sacrifice for sin in order to bring man back to God; was raised from the dead and ascended to God for the purpose of appearing in man's behalf. These claims have never been made of anyone else except Jesus.

By what law shall Jesus be tried to determine his guilt or innocence? First, by the law of Moses under which he lived. Second, by his own teaching which has been universally accepted as the highest law ever given to man. Third, by the standard of purity and holiness agreed on by Jew, Christian, ancient Pagan and modern moralists. He stands before every standard of law known to man, not only not condemned, but sinless. This has been the verdict of friend and foe.

Who shall be called to testify? First, those who knew him personally, both friend and enemy. Second, all who have viewed his life with the most extreme, critical ability.

Judas, who lived with him daily for more than three years, brought back the thirty pieces of silver given for his betrayal, cast it down at the feet of the Jewish rulers, and said, "I have sinned in that I have betrayed innocent blood." (Matt. 27: 3, 4).

Pilate, the Roman Governor, after hearing the conflicting testimony of the Jewish mob, though desiring to find occasion to declare him guilty in order to appease the mob, said, "I find no fault in him." (John 18: 38). Not a word of testimony was given to prove that Jesus had violated either the law of Moses or the civil, Roman law. In all the trials before the council of the Jews and before Pilate, only one charge was sustained: he said he was the Son of God. For that claim, and for none other, he died.

When his Jewish brethren were railing against him, he boldly asked: "Which of you convicteth me of sin?" They were silent.

It is true that on one occasion the Jews charged him with breaking the Jewish Sabbath, but his reply again silenced them. It was only by perverting the meaning of the law of the sabbath that they could so charge him.

For nearly two thousand years the enemies of Jesus have been critically examining his life as set forth in Matthew, Mark, Luke, and John. They have all agreed that the life pictured by his four biographers, when judged by all known standards of purity, present a sinless character. Jesus either lived a sinless life, and these four writers were inspired to picture his life as such, or they conspired to invent and picture a life that was sinless. No other writers in the history of letters have ever been able to picture any other life as sinless, either as fiction or true biography. Therefore, the conclusion is irresistible that the character of the sinless Jesus was real, and that his biographers were guided by the Holy Spirit to accomplish that which never before nor since has been accomplished—the portrayal of a sinless life. This fact alone outweighs all adverse testimony ever given against him.

Peter, one of the twelve, said of him, "Who did no sin, neither was guile found in his mouth." And so testified all who lived with him.

Time and space will permit but one other quotation. The great Emperor, Napoleon, when humbled by defeat, gave utterance from his prison on St. Helena to a speech, so sublime, grand, and inspiring that it is perhaps not surpassed by any uninspired man. Only a few detached sentences can be given here.

"I know men, and I tell you that Jesus Christ is not a man. Superficial minds see a resemblance between Christ and the founders of empires and the gods of other religions. That resemblance does not exist. There is between Christianity and whatever other religion the distance of infinity."

"Paganism is the work of man. One can here read but our imbecility. What do these gods, so boastful, know more than other mortals—these legislators, Greeks or Romans, this Numo, this Lycurgus, these priests of India or of Memphis, this Confucius, this Mohammed? Absolutely nothing. They have made a perfect chaos of morals."

"It is not so with Christ. Everything in him astonishes me. His spirit overawes me, and his will confounds me. Between him and whoever else in the world there is no possible term of comparison. He is truly a being by himself. His ideas and sentiments, the truths which he announces, his manner of convincing, are not explained either by human organization or the nature of things."

"The nearer I approach, the more carefully I examine, everything is above me ..."

"I search in vain in history to find the similar to Jesus

Christ, or anything which can approach the gospel. Neither history, nor humanity, nor the ages, nor nature offer me anything with which I am able to compare to explain it. Here everything is extra-ordinary. The more I consider the gospel, the more I am assured that there is nothing there which is not beyond the march of events, and above the human mind. Even the impious themselves have never dared to deny the sublimity of the gospel, which inspires them with a sort of compulsory veneration."

"In every other existence but that of Christ, how many imperfections?" ("The Messiahship," by Walter Scott, 1860, pp. 153-57).

Let us look into the life of this sinless One. The hour has come for the long expected mediator to be born. As the prophets had foretold that he was to be a king reigning over a universal kingdom, it was expected that he would be born of royal blood in a palace. God's plans were different. The expectant mother was turned away from the village inn because "there was no room." Had the innkeeper but known, the best room would have been given her. What a slighted opportunity! How often may we have turned away the sinless Jesus in the person of some one of the "least of his brethren." The humble but holy Mary goes down to the village stable. How far removed was this from what men regarded as a suitable birthplace for a great king! He came from the greatest heights, from heaven itself, and made his abode in the humblest possible place— a stable. There the Redeemer is born. Look! Listen! Out there on the hills, shepherds are keeping watch over their flocks by night. Behold! The angel of the Lord appears, and the glory of the Lord shines about them. See the shepherds as they fall to the ground trembling with fear. Listen as the angel, in tender tones, speaks to them, "Be not afraid: for behold, I bring to you good tidings of great joy which shall be to all people: For there is born to you this day in the city of David a Saviour, who is Christ the Lord." Look and listen again as there appears a "multitude of the heavenly host praising God, and saying, Glory to God in the highest, and on earth peace, good will to men." God's promise is fulfilled; the Redeemer has come. The mediator between God and a sinful, fallen race is born. A merciful and faithful high priest, who can intercede for us in the immediate presence of God, is here. The prophetic promise, "a body didst thou prepare for me" to be offered willingly to "take away sin" lies quietly in the manger.

In the east the wise men see his star that leads them westward and finally stands over where the young Jesus lies. See them as they present to the infant costly gifts and bow and worship him. What a privilege now to worship him on his throne!

About thirty years later, a young man named John, appears in the wilderness of Judea preaching, saying, "Repent ye; for the kingdom of heaven is at hand." Multitudes hear him, confess their sins and are baptized in Jordan. There is a great throng of people extending far back from the river. We see out there the dense crowd as it parts to make way for one who is coming to John. He comes near. We look anxiously at him. His walk is firm and measured. On his face we see calmness, power, purity. Not a trace of sin mars his serene countenance. He asks John to baptize him. John hesitates. He knows he is baptizing for the "remission of sins," and he knows this young man has no sin to remit. He is perplexed, and says, "I have need to be baptized of thee, and comest thou to me?" "Suffer it to be so now," said Jesus, "for thus it becometh us to fulfill all righteousness." Watch as John leads him out into the river, buries his body in the water, and raises him up from the burial in baptism. "Behold the Spirit of God descending like a dove and coming upon him." Hear the voice of God from heaven, "This is my beloved Son, in whom I am well pleased."

Jesus went immediately into the wilderness where he was tempted by Satan. In the beginning, man was tempted, sinned and fell, was separated from God, and was conquered by death. Jesus came to conquer Satan and to undo his evil work. He was tempted and did not yield. He needed to be "tempted in all points like we yet without sin" to the end "that he might become a merciful and faithful high priest in things pertaining to God," to "be able to succor them that are tempted," and "to make intercession for us."

Let us now go with Jesus to the city of Nain. As he nears

the city, he meets a funeral procession. Funerals are always sad because of the grief of relatives. But this is an unusually sad occasion. It is a young man. It is sad when a promising youth is taken away. Too, he is the son, yes, the only son of a widow. Bereft of her husband, she is now burying her only son, and perhaps her only means of support. How heavy indeed must have been her heart. When the Lord saw her, he had compassion on her, and said unto her, "Weep not." How strange to ask a heart-broken mother to cease weeping when about to bury her only son. But he knew her sorrow would soon be turned to joy. "And he came near and touched the bier; and the bearers stood still. And he said, Young man, I say unto thee, Arise. And he that was dead sat up, and began to speak." Infinite love and sympathy succors the sorrowing widow. Would that we could sincerely believe that, even though seated at God's right hand, he still has the same love and sympathy for us which he had for the widow of Nain.

After a day of toil spent in teaching the people, he said to his disciples, "Let us pass over unto the other side." Being weary, he fell asleep on a pillow in the "hinder part of the ship." A great storm of wind rises. The wind blows violently, the ship tosses, the waves run high and pour into the ship. At first the disciples are not alarmed. Some of them had spent most of their lives along the shore. Doubtless they think the worst will soon be over. But the fury of the wind increases, the waves roll higher, the little ship is filled with water. They are in the greatest danger of going down into the depths of the sea. They are frightened, and rush to the Lord, and cry out in terror, "Master! Master, carest thou not that we perish?" Jesus rises from his pillow. He hears the shrieking of the wind in the rigging, sees the waves as they roll high and spill over the sides, and feels the tossing of the ship, but there is no sign of fright in his face or voice. He knows that his Father "holds the waves in the hollow of his hand." Why should he fear? It was "by him, through him and for him that all things were created." He was there when the earth, wind and sea were called into being. "He rebuked the wind, and said unto the sea, Peace, be still. And the wind ceased, and there was a great calm. And he said unto them, Why are ye fearful? Have ye yet not faith? And they feared exceedingly, and said one to another, Who is this, that even the wind and sea obey him?" And yet when our souls are troubled by our little trials, we "fear exceedingly" because our faith is so weak that we do not fully trust our souls in his keeping.

On another occasion, Jesus is teaching in the temple early one morning. Out toward the entrance we see a commotion. Some scribes and Pharisees are pressing their way through the dense crowd, bringing a prisoner to Jesus. Is it a robber or a murderer? The city is full of such dangerous criminals. No, it is just a poor woman who has made a mistake. They come near to Jesus and tauntingly ask, "Master, Moses commanded that such sinners should be stoned. There is no doubt about her guilt. She was taken in the very act." Why were not both sinners arrested, if one could be? Public sentiment let the man go free just as public sentiment does today. Public sentiment then condemned the woman, the lesser sinner, and excused and set free the man, the greater sinner. Public sentiment today condemns the lesser sinner to social ostracism, while excusing the greater sinner. God has one standard of moral purity for both, but places the greater responsibility on man.

Jesus stoops down and writes on the ground as though he heard them not. "Master, Master, Moses commanded that such as this woman should be stoned. What sayest thou?" Jesus lifted up himself, and said unto them, "He that is without sin among you, let him first cast a stone at her." Again he stooped down and wrote on the ground. In what manner did he utter those words? Did he, in indignation, hiss them through clenched teeth? Or, did he hurl them with the force of a thunderbolt? We are not told, but his words convicted her accusers of being at least as great sinners as she whom they desired to stone. Beginning with the eldest, they went out till the last one was gone. Jesus raised up himself and in pity looked upon the trembling woman. "Woman, where are those thine accusers? hath no man condemned thee?" "No man, Lord." "Neither do I condemn thee: Go and sin no more." Did Jesus mean to encourage her, or anyone now, to sin? A thousand times no! So terrible was sin that he came to die to make an atonement for it. He only meant that it matters not how great one has sinned, or how one may have been cast out and ostracized by men, yet if one repents and turns to God, the past is all blotted out. The love of the sinless Jesus reaches down to the worst sinner offering full pardon if the sins are repented of and forsaken. Of all that Jesus said and did while on earth perhaps nothing makes a stronger appeal to the discouraged, penitent sinner than this story.

There lived in the village of Bethany Mary, Martha, and Lazarus, whom "Jesus loved." Lazarus became seriously sick. And what did the sisters do? Just what we do now when in deep distress. We send for those whom we love most. We want their love and sympathy just as Mary did when in sorrow. They send a hurried messenger over beyond Jordan to tell Jesus, "He whom thou lovest is sick." Jesus tarries two days, then says to his disciples, "Our friend Lazarus sleepeth; but I will go that I may awake him out of sleep." His disciples said, "Lord, if he sleepeth, he will do well." "Then said Jesus to them plainly, Lazarus is dead." The saddest word heard by those in sorrow is that a loved one is "dead." It means that the sparkling eyes, the sweet smile and tender voice will be seen and heard no more. Jesus added, "And I am glad." What? Jesus glad that his friend and the only brother of the sisters is dead? Yes, but for a great reason. "I am glad for your sakes that I was not there, to the intent ye may believe." Yes, and that we who now live may believe that he will come again and call us from the dead to a better life.

There is no fast train, automobile or airplane to take him the long distance. The wearisome journey must be made a step at a time. He nears the home. A messenger brings word to the sisters that the Master is coming. Martha rises from her place of weeping, hurries out, meets Jesus, and, from a broken heart, cries out, "Lord, if thou had been here my brother had not died." She knew Jesus had raised up many from sickbeds, and she is sure had he been here in time he would have healed Lazarus. But now it is too late! Brother has been dead four days already, and since the world began no one has ever lived again after being dead so long. Hear Jesus say to her, "He shall live again." She answers, "I know that he shall live again in the resurrection at the last day." Then it was that Jesus uttered words, the like of which human ears had never before heard. "I am the resurrection and the life." Perhaps this is the strongest assurance that had ever been given of a coming resurrection till that hour.

"Where have ye laid him?" "Lord, come and see." Yes, even the place where the dust of our loved ones lie is sacred. Years ago, in Virginia, I preached much at Laurell Hill. I made my home with Brother Sale, who had two sons, Alva and Frank. Alva, one of the best boys I ever knew, died and was buried over on the hill in the little family burying place. On Sunday morning Brother Sale got his hat and cane, with bowed head, went down the little lane, crossed the main highway, across the little meadow and up the hill. "Where is he going," was my question to Sister Sale. "To Alva's grave. He goes every Sunday morning." As Jesus draws near the tomb, it is recorded, "Jesus wept." Those two words have opened the hearts of countless numbers because it gives us a true picture of the reality of the love of the sinless Jesus. "Behold, how he loved him," said the Jews. "Some of them said, Could not this man, which opened the eyes of the blind, have caused that this man should not have died?"

They arrive at the grave. "Take away the stone," said Jesus. Martha objects, "Lord, by this time the body decayeth; for he hath been dead four days." But the stone is removed. There we see Lazarus, wrapped in his shroud and a napkin about his head. There is no lifting of the chest in respiration; the heart is still. There lies Lazarus, did we say? Yes, but Lazarus is not there. That which we see is only the corruptible house in which Lazarus lived. He is in the paradise of God. When living in Indiana, I was called by wire a long distance to speak at the funeral of Ed Bennett, a fine Christian youth, who had died under the surgeon's knife. The scene was so strongly impressed on my mind that it remains vivid till this day. The father, mother, sister, and seven brothers, stood around that casket, with streaming eyes, as they called, "Ed! Oh, Ed! Speak to us!" But Ed did not speak. He was not there. That which we looked upon was only the earthly house in which Ed had lived. He was in the unseen world.

Someday our loved ones will gather around our old house of clay, and call it by the endearing name of father, mother, brother, sister, son or daughter. But we will not be there, and will not answer to their call.

Jesus offers a short prayer to his Father and then cries with a loud voice, "Lazarus, come forth." At the command of that voice, the blind had seen, the sick had been made whole, the deaf had heard, the winds and waves had obeyed, and here the dead came forth. The day is coming when all the dead will hear that same voice and arise. "Loose him and let him go." Since sin and death entered the world, no such assurance had been given of victory over death and the certainty of a better life. None but the sinless Jesus has ever been able to give such undoubted assurance of a coming resurrection.

"The hour draws near for him to depart out of this world." He observed the Passover with the twelve in a borrowed upper room. This is his last night with them, and being divine, he knew what was the best monument to his memory for those who would afterward love him. He gave thanks separately for a loaf and the cup, "the fruit of the vine," and said, "this is my body . . . this is my blood of the new covenant, which is poured for many unto the remission of sins." "This do in memory of me." No other memorial or monument has ever been seen and observed by so many millions of the most enlightened and righteous as this which was composed of a bit of bread and a cup of the fruit of the vine. It has aided in lifting countless millions to a higher plane of goodness and happiness. It stands between the two greatest events of time, pointing back to the cross where atonement for sin was accomplished and forward to his coming in the clouds to redeem his loved ones, and to give them "a crown of life."

He led them down to the garden of Gethsemane. He left the little company of chosen ones, asked them to pray, went on a little distance, fell on the ground and was very sorrowful, saying, "My soul is exceedingly sorrowful even unto death." He saw before him, not only the torture of the cross, but the shame of his ill treatment. A sensitive person suffers more intensely from shame than from bodily pain. Who can doubt that Jesus' greatest suffering was the shame? So intense was his mental agony that his "sweat became as great drops of blood." Three times he cried out in the anquish of his soul, "Father, if it be possible, let this cup pass away from me: nevertheless, not my will but thine be done." He knew that his mission was to die for the lost, yet when the ordeal of shame and suffering drew near, his soul was greatly troubled, and he prayed for deliverance if there was any other way to save man. His bitter cry was as much to say, "Father, if thy wisdom, power, and love can devise any other way to save man, then Father, save me from this awful shame and death. But, Father, if there is no other way to save man from sin, then let me drink this cup." It was not while before Pilate, nor even on the cross, that his greatest trial of suffering came. It was in the garden. Never before in all his life had he shown any fear, or any hesitation, nor after he came from the garden, did he show any hesitation. Always, except in the garden, he was calm, self-possessed, and without fear. Truly, in the garden of Gethsemane is witnessed the greatest battle of all time.

Although he can ask the Father to send more than twelve legions of angels to rescue him, yet he calmly submits to arrest. His disciples flee in the darkness. The officers bind him as though he were a dangerous criminal, and take him before the highest court of the Jews. False testimony is given against him, but nothing which convicts him of any wrong in their contradictory statements. He is buffeted, spat upon and taunted. Yet, he bears it all in calm silence.

Morning comes and they take him to Pilate, the Roman governor, who alone has the legal authority to impose the sentence the Jews seek—death on the Roman cross. Pilate hears their weak, conflicting testimony, and gives his verdict, "I find no fault in him." With this verdict even Jesus' enemies have agreed to this day. The verdict enrages the Jews, and they become a frenzied mob. Pilate well knows the danger of a general uprising of sedition, and it is his desire to pacify and quiet the leaders if possible. They demand the death sentence and will accept nothing less. Skillful diplomat that he is, Pilate decides on a scheme which he thinks will surely pacify, in a measure, the mob, and also release this "innocent man." It is customary, as a measure of pacifying the Jews, to release at each feast one prisoner of their own choosing. He thinks, in order to make it sure that Jesus can be set free, he will make the choice, not from prisoners in general, but a choice between two only, Jesus and Barabbas, who is guilty of robbery, sedition and murder. "I am, said Pilate, to release unto you at this feast a prisoner whom you may choose. But I now give you your choice between two whom I select. Here is Jesus in whom I find no fault. Here is Barabbas who is guilty of sedition, robbery and murder. Which shall I release?" Surely, thought Pilate, they will not want this noted criminal turned loose and will choose "this innocent man." Pilate was unable to see that here hangs the crisis of a world and its salvation. The current of human events ever since man was lost have converged on this moment. The sinless Jesus on the Roman cross is the only way of redemption. The Scriptures must be fulfilled. The atonement must be made.

Listen to the deafening clamor of the frenzied mob as they cry out in unison, "Release to us Barabbas. Let him incite sedition, rob and murder. Let Jesus' blood be upon our heads." Brother, sister, the wicked Barabbas typifies you and me. The sinless Jesus went to the cross that we sinners might be freed from bondage to sin and death.

He is delivered to the Roman soldiers. They lead him out to Golgotha. There they nail him to the cross. His punishment is not for any sin of his own. "He was despised, and rejected of man; a man of sorrows, and acquainted with grief ... Surely he hath borne our grief and carried our sorrows; yet we did esteem him stricken, smitten of God, and afflicted. But he was wounded for our transgressions, he was bruised for our iniquities; the chastisement of our peace was upon him; and with his stripes we are healed."

For long hours he endures the agony. No earthly friend is there to speak a word of comfort, but his Father is still present with him. At last his Father withdraws his presence and he is left alone. He now cries out in the bitterest grief, "My God, My God, why hast thou forsaken me?" Why did his Father in the last moment withdraw his presence? It was decreed that he should "tread the winepress alone." He alone and unsupported must bear the sins in his own body on the cross.

He bowed his head, and cried, with a loud voice, "Father, into thy hands I commend my spirit." The tragedy of earth and time is ended. Jesus is dead.

Joseph asked Pilate for the body, tenderly removed it from the cross, and laid it in his own new tomb. Do you know that the three days while his body was in the tomb were the darkest and most hopeless of all the days since man sinned? The Redeemer has come, but he now lies in the embrace of death. The only ray of hope during those three days are the three words uttered by him who is now held by the tomb. Those three words are, "I will arise." Can the dead make good his promise? Will the "gates of hades" prevail against his soul, and hold it in the prison house? It is true that David had foreseen, in the person of Jesus, his triumph over death. Speaking in the person of Jesus, he prophesied, "Thou wilt not leave my soul in hades." "It was not possible that he should be holden of death." On the morning of the third day, he conquered death and came forth victorious from the tomb. He met with the apostles on different occasions for about forty days. He led them out on the mountain and gave to them the worldwide commission. He lifted up his hands and blessed them. How their hearts overflowed with joy! Their Master has come back from the dead and is again with them. What their thoughts and ideas in regard to their future with Jesus were, we can never know. But it seems that they still held to the idea that now he would surely proclaim himself king, assemble an army and drive the hated Roman legions out of their country.

While they are looking into his face and listening to his words, a strange thing happens. His feet gently begin to leave the ground, and he, perhaps, slowly rises above their heads. In amazement they watch as his body rises still higher, and at last enters a cloud out of sight. With the speed of light, perhaps, he passes through space till he nears the place where God dwells. The angel porter, watching from the battlement of heaven, cries out: "Lift up your heads O ye gates; and be ye lifted up, ye everlasting doors; and the King of glory shall come in. Who is this King of glory? The Lord of hosts, he is the King of glory." The sinless Jesus swept through the gates that had opened wide and took his seat at the right hand of God, to reign till the last enemy, which is death, shall be destroyed.

What song think you that the angels then sang? May we think, perhaps, that the mighty host of heavenly angels then sang in unison:

> All hail the power of Jesus' name!
>   Let angels prostrate fall,
> Bring forth the royal diadem,
>   And crown him Lord of all.
> Let every kindred, ev'ry tribe,
>   On this terrestial ball,
> To Him all majesty ascribe,
>   And crown him Lord of all.

CHAPTER IX

THE REIGN OF CHRIST
KINGDOM—CHURCH

Christ's throne is in heaven, but the subjects over which he reigns are on earth. The church, which is his spiritual body, is on earth; but he governs it by his law from heaven. The kingdom of Christ and the church are, perhaps, the same in one respect. All the saved through him are citizens in his kingdom, and all the saved through him are members of his spiritual body, the church. Wherever there is one redeemed by Christ, there is a citizen of His kingdom.

One difference between the kingdom and church should be very carefully considered. The kingdom has no form of organization on the earth. Each Christian is a citizen in Christ's kingdom. "So then ye art no more strangers and sojourners, but ye are fellow citizens with the saints, and of the household of God." (Eph. 2:19). The church has a form of organization on the earth which will be considered later.

The beginning and the end of the reign of Christ marks two of the most glorious and inspiring events of time. Daniel foretold the beginning of his reign, and Paul foretells the blessings of the conclusion of his reign.

The Holy Spirit speaking by Daniel said: "And in the days of those kings shall the God of heaven set up a kingdom which shall never be destroyed, nor shall the sovereignty thereof be left to another people, but it shall break in pieces and consume all those kingdoms, and it shall stand for ever." (Dan. 2:44). No kingdom even imagined by man ever compared with that which was prophecied by Daniel. God himself would "set it up," it would fill the earth, break in pieces all other kingdoms, and stand for ever. What must have been his joy in seeing such a glorious kingdom in prophetic vision! How lightly we often appreciate our privileges in being citizens of that kingdom. We are so earth-bound that we fail to see with our eye of faith. The kingdom of Daniel's prophecy is the kingdom that John preached "is at hand." It is the kingdom in which Jesus reigns. He said to Pilate: "My kingdom is not of this world."

On every point of comparison, it is unlike any other kingdom that has ever existed. All other kingdoms have been established and defended by force of arms. Many citizens of other kingdoms have been unwilling subjects ruled by fear. Such kingdoms were limited by the territory in which they existed. All such kingdoms came to an end and were succeeded by others like them.

Jesus was not a king while on the earth. He had no official position; no army to defend him; no money and few friends when most needed, and of course, no kingdom over which to rule.

One thrust of Brutus' dagger ended the life and rule of the Great Ceasar. One last battle sent Napoleon to Saint Helena to die in sorrow. Jesus was crucified on a Roman cross and deserted by his disciples. He was declared risen from the dead before his kingdom was set up and his reign over the lives of the living began. He has never had an unwilling citizen in his kingdom. Only those who willingly offer their hearts and lives in love for him can enter his kingdom. All citizens enter of their own choice, and all who choose, leave his kingdom. No one has ever been held in his kingdom against his will.

Jesus' rule is by love. He seeks only the good and happiness of his citizens. But too often Christians seem to think he has imposed arbitrary rules to deny them some things they love and to impose upon them duties hard to bear. He denies them only such things as bring unhappiness in this life and imposes only such things as bring happiness. The whole purpose of Christ is to revelop characters that are fitted for life eternal with the angels in heaven. That is why his "yoke is easy and his burden is light."

In times past, kings were crowned that they might begin their reign with pomp and splendor. Even our own elected presidents are inaugurated with much show and glamour. How different was the crowning of Jesus as king, and his beginning to reign in the hearts of man. There was no previous announcement of the day, and no parade to get applause from the multitude. The event came as a surprise to his few chosen friends. They had scarcely enough faith to "tarry in the city, until they were clothed with power from on high."

A great crowd was gathered in Jerusalem, but they were there to keep the Passover. The Holy Spirit was poured out on the apostles, Christ's chosen witnesses. Cloven tongues like as of fire sat upon each of them. Peter stood up with the eleven and declared that this was that which Joel had foretold: "And it shall come to pass in the last days, saith God, I will pour forth of my Spirit upon all flesh—And it shall be, that whosoever shall call on the name of the Lord shall be saved." (Acts 2:17-21). The scene on Pentecost was perhaps the most wonderful sight ever to be observed by men.

The crowning of Jesus in heaven, when he was given his throne at the right hand of God, certainly was not like anything on earth.

The day of Pentecost was the greatest day since the fall of man. On that day, Jesus was declared risen from the dead, and seated on his throne in heaven. On that day, sinners were commanded for the first time to render obedience to Jesus. Full remission of sins was promised for the first time. About three thousand were told to repent and be baptized for the remission of sins. On that day, the Kingdom of God—the church—was set up. The "little stone cut out without hands" was to become a great mountain and fill the whole earth. (Daniel 2). The privilege of becoming citizens in that kingdom is the greatest blessing that can be enjoyed in this life. "Wherefore, also God hath highly exalted him, and give unto him the name which is above every name; that at the name of Jesus every knee should bow, of things in heaven and things under the earth, and that every tongue should confess that Jesus Christ is Lord, to the glory of God the Father." (Phil. 2:9-11).

On the day of Pentecost, Christ began to reign as king in heaven, and on that day, the church was established on earth in Jerusalem. On that day, the apostles announced that Jesus was risen from the dead, and was enthroned in heaven. Hearers were convicted of sin and cried, "Men and brethren what shall we do?" Peter, guided by the Holy Spirit, said: "Repent, ye and be baptized everyone of you in the name of Jesus Christ unto the remission of your sins; and ye shall receive the gift of the Holy Spirit." About three thousand gladly were baptized. Those baptized formed the church of our Lord. Of that church he had said: "On this rock I will build my church, and the gates of hades shall not prevail against it." (Matt. 16:18). "And they continued steadfastly in the apostles' teaching and in fellowship, in the breaking of bread, and in prayers." (Acts 2:42). This is the record of the establishing of the church of the Lord on the earth and of its worship. It is so plain and easy to understand that none who desires to know how to be added to the church and to worship as the Bible teaches needs to be led into an association or form of worship displeasing to the Lord.

The whole church, or as some prefer to say, the church universal, does not have an earthly organization. It has no earthly head of authority over all Christians. Catholics claim that the Pope with the cabinet of cardinals are authorized to rule over all believers in Christ. Denominations assume the right to form creeds and enact laws to govern all whom they can influence to submit to their assumed authority. Many are involved in such unscriptural organizations while in infancy.

It is not so in the New Testament church—the body of which Christ is head. Speaking of the church as a whole group, the Holy Spirit says there is "one body (church), even as there is one Lord, one faith, one hope, one Spirit, one God." (Eph. 4).

The only form of organization that the Lord authorizes is the local congregation, with elders or overseers, and deacons. Preachers, or, as often called, evangelists, cannot be called officers of the church. Their work is not to rule, but to "preach the word: be urgent in season, out of season: reprove, rebuke, exhort with all long-suffering and teaching." (II Timothy 4:2). The work of elders is to oversee and "guide the flock." They are not dictators, nor a board to decide matters by majority vote. (We are sorry we cannot continue the work of elders in this writing).

The local congregation, or church, is the only organization

organized by Christ. Any organization or group of Christians larger or smaller, or different from the local church is in rebellion against Christ. No other organization than the local church can be governed by the "perfect law of liberty." Whether the laws are written or unwritten rules of management, such as in opposition to the New Testament pattern of the Lord's church.

The church is the greatest work God has done for man. The earth and all that it contains was planned and created for man's temporal good. The church was purposed in Christ before the foundation of the world. It will end with the close of time. It was conceived in God's love. His wisdom planned it, and his power formed it. Its design is the redemption of a fallen race that it might be reconciled to God, and brought at last to God's habitation.

Through and by the church the gospel is to be preached, and the widows and orphans cared for. In the days of the inspired apostles, there was no other organization to supplant the church in fulfilling its mission. Individual Christians preached the gospel and ministered to needy as their opportunity and ability enabled them to do so. Even to intimate that the church as the Lord established is not sufficient for Christians to do all that God wants done is to impeach the wisdom and power of God. The Holy Spirit has specifically told us that every scripture inspired of God is "that the man of God be complete, furnished completely unto every good work." (II Tim. 3:17). The Holy Spirit by Peter says: "According as his divine power hath given unto us all things that pertain to life and godliness." (II Peter 1:3). He says by Paul to the Colossians, "And ye are complete in him, which is the head of all principalities and power." (Col. 2:10). Why quote more of the many like declarations of the Holy Spirit? If we will not believe God when he speaks once, we will not believe him if he speaks a thousand times. "Christ also loved the church, and gave himself up for it; that he might sanctify it, having cleansed it by the washing of water with the word, and that he might present the church to himself a glorious church, not having spot or wrinkle or any such thing; but that it should be holy and without blemish." (Eph. 5:26, 27).

How long Christ's reign will continue, we do not know. Many have set the date in years past, but his reign continues. The time when he is to come is known to God only. Our concern is to watch and be ready for his coming.

Paul says: "But now hath Christ been raised from the dead, the firstfruits of them that are asleep. For since by man came death, by man came also the resurrection of the dead. For as in Adam all die, so also in Christ shall all be made alive. But each in his own order; Christ the firstfruits; then they that are Christ's at his coming. Then cometh the end, when he shall deliver up the kingdom to God, even the Father; when he shall have abolished all rule and all authority and power. For he must reign, till he hath put all his enemies under his feet. The last enemy that shall be abolished is death—And when all things have been subjected unto him, then shall the Son himself be subjected to him that did subject all things unto him, that God may be all in all." (I Cor. 15).

CHAPTER X

HOW TO BECOME A CHRISTIAN

(NOTE: Reprint from book of Sermons by the author, 1909).

"See, here is water; what doth hinder me to be baptized?" (Acts 8:36).

There is probably more diversity of opinion concerning the answer to the question: "Who is a Christian?" than on any other pertaining to the religion taught in the New Testament. Yet, there should be no confusion about the matter, for God declared that the way would be so plain that "wayfaring men, though fools, shall not err therein." (Isa. 35:8).

No one can possibly know that he is a Christian until he has first learned how to become a Christian. God has not only told us how to become Christians, followers of Christ, but he has also shown us how others became followers of Christ when guided by inspired preachers. In the eighth chapter of Acts of Apostles, there is an inspired historical account of how the Treasurer of Queen Candace became a follower of Christ. The account is brief, but it is complete and clear. The one who led this man to the Savior was supernaturally guided by the Spirit, hence made no mistake in the instructions he gave the man who became a Christian. The record of this event was made by an inspired pen also. When we learn how he became a Christian, we will then know how people must become Christians now.

When we are first introduced to this Ethiopian officer, he was not a Christian, not a follower of Christ, not in the church or kingdom. His sins had not been remitted; he was not saved. But, when we part company from him, he is a Christian, a child of God; he has been "translated out of the kingdom of darkness into the kingdom of God's dear Son;" his sins have been remitted; he is saved from past sins; he is "going on his way rejoicing." When we learn what he heard, believed and obeyed in order to be pardoned, saved, and to become a child of

God, we will know what people must hear, believe and obey now in order to enjoy the same blessings. The same gospel that he heard, believed and obeyed was to be preached to the "whole creation," and to continue to be in force till the close of the gospel age. There has been no change made in the gospel, the church, or in the terms of pardon, or law of induction into the church. People must receive the remission of their sins, be saved, enter the church now just as this man was saved and entered the church. The church and the terms of admission into it are unchanged and unchangeable.

What, then, did this man hear, believe and obey to be saved or to become a Christian?

There were four persons, or personages, that are mentioned in the inspired account: the angel of the Lord; the Holy Spirit; Philip the inspired preacher; and the Ethiopian officer. What did each one do? What relation does the work of each have to people now?

The angel, or messenger, of the Lord was the first party to act. To whom did God send the angel? Did he send him to the Ethiopian officer to tell him that, because he was a sincere worshippers (he was returning from Jerusalem where he had been to worship under the law of Moses), he was already saved and accepted with the Lord? He did not. Did God send the angel to the sinner to tell him what to do to be saved? No, he did not send the angel to the sinner at all in this case. God had committed the work of preaching the gospel to man, and did not take it out of their hands and commit it to angels.

He did send an angel to Cornelius who was a devout man, prayed always, and "gave much alms to the people." But the angel did not tell Cornelius that, because he was sincere, prayed and gave alms to the people, he was saved. Neither did the angel tell him what to do in order to be saved. He told him to "send men to Joppa and call for one Simon, who is surnamed Peter," and "he shall tell thee what thou oughtest to do," or "words whereby thou and thy house shall be saved." (Acts 10:16; 11:14). When the Savior talked with Paul, near Damascus, Paul cried out: "Lord, what wilt thou have me to do?" Jesus did not tell him what to do but said: "Arise, and go into the city, and it shall be told thee what thou must do." He went into the city. The Lord sent an inspired preacher who told him what he "must do," and he obeyed immediately. God, through Christ, had committed the work of preaching into the hands of men, and Jesus himself, when talking with Paul, did not take it out of their hands and tell Paul what he must do to be saved.

"The angel of the Lord spake unto Philip, saying, Arise, and go toward the south unto the way that goeth down from Jerusalem unto Gaza, which is desert." Philip at once obeyed the command. He saw the Ethiopian officer returning from Jerusalem where he had been to worship according to the law given from Mount Sinai. He was either a Jew or a convert to the law and form of worship which God had given to the Jews through Moses, and did not know that Jesus had "fulfilled it," "taken it out of the way," "nailed it to the cross," and had "become the end of the law to all that believe." (Rom. 10: 4; Col. 2:14). He was a devout, sincere worshiper, but he was not saved. He was still trying to approach God through Moses as mediator, and to serve God under the old covenant. He did not know that Christ is now mediator of a "better covenant, with better promises" that has taken the place of the old covenant. (Heb. 8:5-13).

The Holy Spirit now takes part in turning this man to Christ. To whom does God send the Spirit? Does he send him directly into the heart of the sinner who is to be turned to Christ, convert him directly, and make him a child of God? No, the Holy Spirit was not sent into the sinner's heart at all. The Spirit was sent to Philip, the inspired preacher. How did the Spirit influence Philip? Did he move him by impressions or emotional feelings that were mysterious and indefinable? He most certainly did not move Philip by mere emotions or feelings. The Spirit "said unto Philip, Go near, and join thyself to this chariot." The Spirit influenced Philip by words addressed to his understanding. Philip heard the words and obeyed them. This is the only way, so far as we are informed in the Word of God, that the Holy Spirit has ever influenced anyone, except by miracles addressed to the eye to confirm the word spoken. The Holy Spirit has always moved people to obedience by words spoken or written by inspired prophets and apostles. When people heard the words spoken or written by inspired men, they heard the words of the Holy Spirit. When people were influenced or moved to obedience by the words of the Holy Spirit spoken by inspired preachers of the gospel, they were influenced or moved by the Holy Spirit. When they resisted the words spoken by inspired preachers, they resisted the Holy Spirit. The Jews heard the word of the Holy Spirit as spoken through Stephen, and "resisted" or opposed his words. The Spirit by the mouth of Stephen said to them: "Ye stiff-necked and uncircumsized in heart and ears, ye do always resist the Holy Spirit as your fathers did, so do ye." (Acts 6:51). When people hear the written words of the apostles now, they hear the words of the Holy Spirit. When people are now influenced or moved to obedience by the written words of the inspired apostles, they are influenced or moved to obedience by the Holy Spirit. When people now resist or oppose the written word of the apostles, they resist the Holy Spirit just as the Jews did.

Philip "ran" to the chariot and heard the Ethiopian officer reading the following from the prophecy of Isaiah: "He was led as a sheep to the slaughter; and like a lamb dumb before his shearer, so he opened not his mouth: in his humiliation his judgment was taken away: and who shall declare his generation? for his life is taken from the earth." Philip asked him if he understood what he read, and he said: "How can I except some man should guide me?" He then asked Philip, saying, "I pray thee, of whom speaketh the prophet this? of himself, or of some other man?" No doubt he knew something of the persecutions of Isaiah, and thought that possibly he was describing his own sufferings. He desired to know whether he was telling of his own sufferings or prophesying of someone else. What did Philip do? He had but one for an audience. Suppose that Philip had been as easily cast down and discouraged as many preachers of our time by reason of small audiences. He could not have done much preaching. Today, some of us must wait till we get a considerable audience before we risk delivering any of our "best sermons." If we arrive at the appointed place for preaching and find but a few present, we usually feel that we need only to make a "little talk" and dismiss the people. If the audience happens to be large, then we feel that it is a good opportunity to deliver one of our best sermons and make a favorable impression. How far short we are from apostolic example in earnestness and willingness to teach an audience of one. When we imitate the example of the first preachers and individual Christians, and make a wholehearted effort to turn individuals, rather than whole audiences, to Christ, then we will accomplish much more than we are now doing.

"Philip opened his mouth and began at the same scripture and preached unto him Jesus." He told him that Jesus was the one of whom Isaiah had spoken these words, and that he had recently fulfilled the prophecy. But what did he preach? This man was an unbeliever in the Sonship of Jesus, and it was necessary to preach to him enough of the life and words of Jesus so that he might believe on him. Paul says: "So then faith cometh by hearing." (Rom. 10:17). John says: "These things (signs or miracles) are written that ye might believe that Jesus is the Christ, the Son of God; and that believing ye might have life through his name." (John 20:31). Had some of the modern clergymen, or so-called evangelists, been in Philip's place, they would no doubt, have waxed eloquent in telling him of "our Church," "the soundness of our creed," of the "large numbers we have," of "our great missionary societies," of "our institutions of learning," and thus have tried to influence him to "join our church." But, fortunately, for us, Philip was concerned only that the man might be turned to Christ, might put him on, become a child of God, receive the remission of sins, and be "added to the Lord." In order to accomplish this result, he simply preached to him the gospel. In order that he might believe on Christ, he must tell of Christ's life and works sufficiently to produce faith in him. Philip needed to tell him of the miraculous birth of Jesus in Bethlehem of Judea, how he came to John and demanded baptism at his hands in order to "fulfill all righteousness," how John took him down into the Jordan, buried him beneath the liquid wave, and how, as he came up out of the water, the "heavens were opened, and the Spirit descended like a dove and abode upon him." He must tell him how Jesus opened the eyes of the blind, gave hearing to the deaf, healed the sick, cleansed the leper, raised the dead, and stilled the winds and waves. Finally he must tell him how Jesus was given a mock trial, condemned to die, nailed to the cross on Calvary's hill, and buried in Joseph's tomb. He must tell him that, on the third day, He burst the bars of death, came forth from the grave, mingled with his disciples forty days, led them out on the mount, lifted up his hands, blessed them, and gave them the great commission that is as broad as the earth and as long as time— the commission which extends to every creature and will remain in force till the end of the world. Finally, he must tell him how Jesus ascended to heaven and was "seated on the right hand of God."

What effect did the preaching of Jesus have on this man? The same effect that it always has on honest-hearted people. It made him a believer in Christ, and caused him to desire to obey him and be saved.

But suppose that he had been as self-satisfied and sensitive as many religious people of our day. What effect would Philip's preaching have had on him? He would have become offended and refused to listen to him. Judging from the manner in which many people now talk and act, he would probably have answered Philip after the following manner: "If what you have preached is true, then I am not a saved man. But I want you to understand that I have been to Jerusalem to worship according to the law that God gave through Moses. I know I am right because I feel that I am. Why, when I was in Jerusalem I heard about you *Nazarenes*. You are spoken against everywhere. Your people are poor, ignorant, and there are only a few of you. You think everybody else is wrong but you. I would hate to be as narrow-minded as you people are. I believe in charity. 'Let every man be fully persuaded in his own mind'." But this man was honest, sincere, and willing to listen to the word of God. When he learned that he needed to obey the gospel in order to be saved, he did not hesitate. He did not ask, "What will become of my parents or grandparents who never heard the gospel." Neither did he ask, "What will become of the Jews who have not obeyed the gospel?"

"As they went on their way, they came unto a certain water: and the Eunuch said, See, here is water; what doth hinder me to be baptized?" Let us pause here and consider the question very carefully. Perhaps we may think there are some things in the record that are not true, and perhaps there are some things recorded in Philip's answer to this question that you have never carefully considered. Let us be as sincere, honest, as willing to learn the will of the Lord, and as ready to obey it as this man was. We must be as honest and as willing to learn and obey the will of the Lord as he was in order to be accepted by the Lord.

Suppose you should start out tomorrow and visit a number of religious teachers of the present day, and ask each the question, "What hinders me to be baptized?" What would be the answer? Would all religious teachers give the same answer? We know that they would not. There would be nearly as many different answers as the religious teachers visited. What are some of the answers that would be received? I once saw two girls, about fourteen and fifteen years old, come forward in a meeting conducted by two preachers and demand baptism. The preachers brought them before the congregation and asked them a long list of questions. I distinctly remember two of them. One was: "Will you obey the rules of our church?" The other was: "Will you pledge yourselves (two young girls) that you will not take up arms and go to war?"

I once knew a young man who went forward in a meeting and desired to be baptized. The preacher in charge (who told me the story) had him to relate his "experience," then called for a vote of the members present as to whether he should be baptized. A majority, among them the preacher, voted against baptizing him. Thus he was refused an opportunity to obey the Lord.

Again, ask religious teachers the question, "What hinders me to be baptized?" and they will ask you how you feel. They will ask, "Do you feel that God, for Christ's sake, has pardoned your sins? Do you feel that the burden of sin and guilt has been rolled away, and that you are saved and a child of God?" If the one desiring baptism can give answers satisfactory to the religious instructors, they will baptize him, but if the answers are not satisfactory, the penitent sinner will be refused baptism in obedience to Christ.

Again, ask a large number of religious instructors the question, "What hinders me to be baptized?" and they will answer, "You must first pray, and be prayed for, for the pardon of your sins. Give up all, earnestly pray, and we will pray for you till God pardons your sins. Then, we will baptize you." If the anxious inquirer accepts the instructions of these religious teachers, then will begin a time of prayer. God will be entreated to "send down converting power" separate and apart from the gospel to convert and save the penitent sinner. He will be urged to pray to God to pardon his sins till God pardons him. His teachers will promise him pardon and salvation solely upon the conditions of faith, repentance and prayer.

We must pause here long enough to make a few statements, for I do not want to be misunderstood. Unless the sinner believes with his whole heart, repents and is praying with his whole heart, he is in no condition to render an acceptable obedience to the Lord. Without the proper degree of faith and repentance and the proper condition of heart, one might be immersed a thousand times and his sins would not be remitted. Paul said to the brethren at Rome, "But ye obeyed from the heart that form of doctrine which was delivered unto you, being then made free from sin, ye became the servants of righteousness," and "have your fruit unto holiness, and the end everlasting life." (Rom. 6: 17, 22). It has been charged that members of the church of Christ teach that just so one is immersed in water, his sins are remitted, regardless of his faith and repentance. This is a gross misrepresentation. New Testament Christians teach that baptism can be acceptable to the Lord only if it be "obedience from the heart." Paul says that the sinner is "made free from sin" when he obeys this "form of doctrine from the heart." The proper degree of faith and repentance and the right condition of heart must precede obedience. On the other hand, an individual might claim to believe with his whole heart, to have repented in the bitterest degree, and refuse to obey the commandment of Jesus to be baptized. For such an individual there is not one word of promise in the Word of God. Such a one might stand still and pray and be prayed for till his dying day, yet, if he refuses to obey the Lord, there is not one syllable of promise for him. When the sinner believes and repents with his whole heart, he will pray. There is no power that can keep him from praying. But God does not command the alien sinner, who has never obeyed the gospel, to pray for pardon, or to pray for the forgiveness of his alien sins. No inspired apostle ever commanded the sinner before he had first obeyed the commandment to be baptized to pray for pardon. The inspired apostles never prayed to God to "send converting power" into the heart of the sinner. The gospel is the "power of God unto salvation." The work of the apostles was to preach the gospel earnestly to sinners and to urge them to obey it. Read carefully the history of the preaching of the inspired apostles and teachers beginning with the day of Pentecost—when Peter preached the first sermon after Christ had been crucified, raised from the dead, ascended to heaven and crowned at the right hand of God—and continuing until the New Testament closes, and you will not find an example of any inspired preacher either teaching the sinner to stand still and pray for pardon or praying for God to pardon sinners without obedience to the gospel. What is the difference between that which so-called evangelists and teachers tell the alien sinner and what God says to the sinner who believes and repents with his whole heart? Modern preachers and teachers tell sinners who have never obeyed the Lord to wait and pray for pardon, and that the evidence of salvation will be the feeling that their sins are pardoned. Where is the proof for this statement? That modern teachers tell sinners who have never obeyed the Lord to wait and pray for pardon is general knowledge. This is practiced in almost every community. But when inspired preachers found people believing, repenting and praying, what did they command such to do? As Paul journeyed toward Damascus, a light shone around him; he fell to the earth and the Lord spoke to him. "Who art thou, Lord?" was Paul's inquiry. "I am Jesus, whom thou persecuteth," was the answer of Jesus. "Paul, trembling and astonished, said, Lord, what wilt thou have me to do?" "Go into the city," said the Lord, "and there it shall be told thee what thou must do." Paul arose from the earth and went into the city. So sincere was his penitence that he refused to eat or drink. He prayed and was without food for three days. The Lord sent Ananias to him. He found Paul as strong a believer, as penitent in heart, and as earnest in prayer as any man who ever lived. Suppose that some of the noted modern evangelists or religious teachers had been present. What would they have said to Paul? They, no doubt, would either have assured him that his sins were already pardoned, and urged him to arise and "give glory to God," or they would have exhorted him to continue to pray to God to pardon him. The modern preacher would also himself have prayed to God to pardon and save this penitent believer. Paul would have been assured that when God pardoned him he would "feel it," and know from his feelings that he was saved. But, fortunately, no preacher of the modern kind visited Paul. God sent to him an inspired preacher, one who was supernaturally guided by the Holy Spirit. What did this inspired preacher tell Paul, a penitent, praying believer, to do? He said: "And now why tarriest thou? Arise, and be baptized, and wash away thy sins, calling on the name of the Lord." (Acts 10: 1-18; 22: 16). The apostles were commanded to "go into all the world and preach the gospel to every creature." The Holy Spirit was bestowed upon them to "guide them into all truth," and "to bring all things to their remembrance" that Jesus had commanded them. They went forth and preached Christ and him crucified. People heard what they preached, believed on Christ as the Son of God, and cried out: "Men and brethren, what shall we do?" The Holy Spirit speaking through Peter, answered, "Repent and be baptized everyone of you in the name of Jesus Christ unto the remission of sins." The result was recorded thus: "They that gladly received his word were baptized." (Acts 2: 37, 38). Modern preachers teach believing, penitent, praying sinners to stand still and pray for pardon. God commands them to arise and obey for pardon. Those who believe, repent, stand still and pray, and refuse to obey the Lord, obey the commandment of men; hence they rely upon the promise of men for salvation. Those who believe, repent, and in a prayerful condition of heart, obey the Lord in baptism, rely upon God's promise for salvation. The one class builds upon the sand, the other class builds upon the rock. (Matt. 7:24, 25).

But what did the Holy Spirit, speaking through Philip, tell the Ethiopian officer hindered him, or might hinder him, from being baptized? What the Holy Spirit spoke through this inspired preacher is infallible, and is as binding as though God himself spoke directly to persons now. Philip answered and said: "If though believest with all thine heart thou mayest." He did not ask him how he felt, what he had experienced, or what he had dreamed. He did not pledge him to "obey the rules of our Church." Neither did he bring him before the church, have him relate an "experience," nor take a vote to determine whether he was fit to be baptized. He did not pray to God to pardon his sins, or tell the sinner to pray to God for pardon. Philip, being inspired, knew that God was always ready and anxious to pardon every sinner who would "obey from the heart the form of doctrine delivered them." (Rom. 6:17-21). The officer did not hear Philip read from a humanly-devised creed a list of questions, and a list of answers for him to repeat after him. The officer simply said: "I believe that Jesus Christ is the Son of God." Was this confession necessary? Was it all the confession that God had commanded? Paul says: "For with the heart man believeth unto righteousness, and with the mouth confession is made unto salvation." (Rom. 10:8-10). This declaration is sufficient to show that God requires a confession to be made. But is this the confession that is made "unto salvation?" In Romans 10: 9, Paul says: "If thou shalt confess with thy mouth the Lord Jesus, and shalt believe in thine heart that God raised him from the dead, thou shalt be saved." Jesus said: "Whosoever therefore shall confess me before men, him will I confess also before my Father who is in heaven." (Matt. 10:32). Peter confessed the Savior by saying: "Thou are the Christ, the Son of the living God." (Matt. 16:16). The only confession that is authorized by command or example is to confess: "I believe that Jesus is the Christ, the Son of the living God." Is this confession sufficient? It is all that the Lord has commanded.

When the Ethiopian officer made this confession, Philip

did not hesitate any longer. There was no waiting to administer any further "baptismal vows." "And he commanded the chariot to stand still; and they went down into the water, both Philip and the Eunuch; and he baptized him." We need to pause here long enough to clear away some of the rubbish and remove some of the objects that men have thrown around the divine record.

1. It is argued that there is no evidence in the record that the eunuch was immersed. It is said that "into" does not necessarily mean "entirely in" that which is mentioned, but that it may mean "to, at, or nearby." But let us see. The word of the Lord says they "came unto a certain water." That certainly places them to the water, at, or near the water. Then the record says they went still further. Went where? "Went down into the water," and "came up out of the water." Did you ever notice the words "down," and "up," in the record here? If they "came unto the water" and "went down into the water," who can doubt that they were actually entirely in the water? Suppose evidence were being given in a modern court of law, and the statement was made that certain persons "came unto a river," "went down into the river," and "came up out of the river." Would such evidence be accepted to prove that the persons mentioned were actually "in" the river? To doubt or question such clear and explicit evidence would be regarded as beyond all reason. Why did God inspire the divine writer to put in the record the words "down" and "up?" Doubtless he foresaw how people in our day would try to confuse the minds of the people, and he wanted to make it so clear that no one could fail to see the truth. You can never get "in" water without "going down," and you can never get out of water without "coming up."

2. It is objected that there is no evidence that the Ethiopian officer was immersed, because we can't know certainly, it is claimed, who it was that "went down" and came "up." It is argued that possibly a servant may have been sent down to bring some water up to the chariot, which Philip sprinkled on the man to be baptized. The careful reader will observe that there is no mention of any servant being present on this occasion. Two men only are metioned, Philip and the eunuch

—the preacher and the man to be baptized. There were no attendants or servants with the Ethiopian officer, or God, in his wisdom, did not mention them. But who "went down into the water," and "came up out of the water?" Was it the preacher and the man to be baptized, or was it some one else? Listen to the record: "They went down into the water, both Philip and the eunuch, and he baptized him." I think this is the most remarkably explicit statement that I have ever examined, even in the Bible. Five words are used in one short sentence stating that it was the preacher and candidate to be baptized who went down into the water. First, the pronoun "they" is used which must refer to the only two persons mentioned in the record; second and third "both" and "both" again refers to the only two who are mentioned in the narrative; and, their names are separately called, "Philip and the eunuch," and fifth, "he" and "him," can only refer to the two men mentioned in the narrative. Is it now possible to doubt that the preacher and the man to be baptized actually "went down into the water," and "came up out of the water." They who doubt it are without the pale of reason, cannot be influenced by the plainest facts, and are incapable of believing on the clearest possible testimony.

3. It is further objected, that this man could not have been immersed because they were in a desert where there was no water. What was desert? Not the whole country between Jerusalem and Gaza, but Gaza was a desert, or deserted place. The country for some distance from Jerusalem was very fertile and well-watered. Who knows how far they were from Jerusalem? But laying all that aside, was there a "certain water," in that part of country where Philip baptized the Ethiopian officer? In the first place, if you will examine any small map usually found in the back of ordinary Bibles, you will find at least four water courses laid down, even on a map no larger than four by six inches in size. Some maps give a larger number of water courses between Jerusalem and Gaza. It is shown to be a well-watered country. But, above all, the word of God says "there was a certain water," that they "came unto it," "went down into it," that while they were in it, Philip baptized the penitent believer who had confessed his faith in Christ, and that "they came up out of the water." With all this array

of the clearest possible testimony from modern maps and the word of God that there was a "certain water," one who still argues that there was no water there does not need water for baptism; he is not ready for it. All the water in the world could do him no good religiously. He might be immersed a thousand times and it would avail him nothing in the sight of God. It is not baptism that he needs, but faith in the word of God. Till he believes what God plainly declares, he need not be concerned about baptism. Baptism is for the believer, those who have "set to their seal that God is true."

How was the Ethiopian baptized? By what "mode" did Philip administer baptism? This is a question frequently asked. Do you know, my friend, that such a thing as "modes" of baptism is not mentioned in the word of the Lord? All this talk about "modes" of baptism is unknown to the word of God.

But, says one, "Learned men differ, and how am I to know who is right? How am I to be certain to make no mistake? Should I have water sprinkled on me? Or should I be immersed?" My friend, there is not the least excuse for the earnest, honest, inquirer to make a mistake if he will only decide the matter according to common sense and the word of God.

Suppose that A sells to B a farm for $1,000. The day arrives when the deed is to be delivered by A, and B is to pay over his $1,000 in exchange for the deed—his title to the farm. Mr. B addresses Mr. A as follows: "Mr. B, I have filled out two forms of deed, and I will sign the one you choose. Deed No. 1 fills every requirement of the laws of this state to the last syllable. Every legal authority in the state declares that this form of deed will stand the test of every court. Every purchaser of real estate is willing to accept it. No one who has ever accepted this form of deed has ever been know to become dissatisfied with it, and wanted to exchange it for form No. 2. Here is No. 2: It was gotten up by some of the most learned lawyers in the state. They think it will stand the test of every court. Many people are purchasing large tracts of real estate and accepting this form of deed. But, there are a large number of legal authorities who claim this form No. 2 does not fill all the requirements of the laws of our state, and they do not think it will stand the test of the courts, especially the Supreme Court. There are many purchasers of real estate who will not accept this form of deed at all, and there are many who hold real estate under it who are doubtful about its standing the test of the Supreme Court. Besides, thousands who have first accepted deed form No. 2 have become dissatisfied with it, and exchanged it for deed No. 1. But no one is known to have accepted deed No. 1, become dissatisfied and exchanged it for deed No. 2. Now, Mr. B, I will execute your choice. Which do you prefer? Form No. 1, that all authorities say will stand the final test, and every one is satisfied with, or deed No. 2, that many authorities say will not stand the test in court, and thousands have become dissatisfied with, and exchanged for deed No. 1." Friend, a thousand dollars is at stake. Which form of deed will Mr. B. accept? Even a child will say that he will accept the deed that all agree is safe. Deed No. 1 represents immersion, and deed No. 2 represents sprinkling and pouring. If everyone would exercise the same concern when obeying the command of the Lord as they do when a thousand dollars is involved, not one would ever accept sprinkling or pouring for baptism. Thousands who have had water sprinkled or poured on them for baptism are now living in doubt and dissatisfaction. Multitudes have become so dissatisfied that they have renounced their sprinkling and have been immersed. Many have died and gone into eternity doubting and dissatisfied in regard to their obedience. Should you not exercise the same care and common sense in securing to yourself a well-founded hope of eternal life as you do when a thousand dollars is involved? You cannot afford to take such risks when your soul is to be saved or lost.

Let us now look at the question of baptism from the New Testament point of view. It need not concern you very much as to what learned men may have said, or now say, on this question. I will only remark that all authorities of any note, even those who have practiced sprinkling and pouring for baptism, unite in saying that the primary meaning of the Greek word baptizo, from which we have the word baptize, means to "dip, plunge, immerse." But the Lord knew that the great mass of people would not be able to examine the question in the original Greek language—the language in which the New

Testament was first written. Therefore, God has made the meaning of baptism so plain that anyone may know, beyond a shadow of doubt, when he has obeyed the Lord. The references to baptism are so numerous and clear that one need not be in doubt a single day. Let us now arrange them—immersion in one column, and sprinkling in another—and compare and contrast each with the word of the Lord. Examine carefully the following diagram and the scriptures indicated:

IMMERSION REQUIRES	SPRINKLING REQUIRES :
1. Water.	1. Water.
2. Going to water.	2. They bring water to them.
3. Much water.	3. Little water.
4. G o i n g down into the water.	4. They bring water up.
5. A burial.	5. No form of burial.
6. A planting.	6. No form of planting.
7. The body washed.	7. The body is not washed.
8. A birth of water.	8. No birth of water.
9. A resurrection.	9. No resurrection.
10. C o m i n g up out of the water.	10. No coming up out of the water.

By comparing and contrasting sprinkling and pouring with immersion, we see that they are alike on one point only: water is required in both. But the two practices are directly the reverse of each on nine points of the ten. If immersion is baptism, then sprinkling and pouring cannot possibly be baptism. They are contrary to each other. What does the New Testament require in order to obey this command? Let us examine the following diagram:

1. Water. Acts 10:47; 8:36; John 3:23.
2. Going to water. Matt. 3:5; Mark 1:5-9; Acts 8:36-57.
3. Much water. John 3:23.
4. Going down into water. Acts 8:38.
5. A burial. Rom. 6:4-5; Col. 2:12.
6. A form of planting. Rom. 6:5.
7. The body washed. Heb. 10:22.
8. A birth of water. John 3:5.
9. A resurrection. Rom. 6:5; Col. 3:1.

10. Coming up out of the water. Matt. 3:16; Mark 1:10; Acts 8:39.

Thus it is clearly seen that immersion fills all ten of the New Testament requirements, just as the fingers of the two hands fit together, while sprinkling or pouring fills one requirement and is directly contradictory to the word of God in nine points of the ten. Those who have believed on the Lord with their whole hearts, repented of their sins, confessed with their mouths that Jesus is the Christ, the Son of God, and, then, have gone to the water, down into the water, been buried in baptism, had their bodies washed, been born of water, raised from baptism, and have come up out of the water, have without the least doubt obeyed from the heart the "form of doctrine" contained in the gospel. Hence, they have been "made free from sin," "become the servants of righteousness," and have become the children of God. There is no promise in the gospel for those who have not obeyed the plain requirements of the word of God. They have not "put on Christ." (Gal. 3:27.) They are not children of God. Why? They have not been "born of water and the Spirit."

"When they came up out of the water, the Spirit of the Lord caught away Philip, and the Eunuch saw him no more; and he went on his way rejoicing." Why did the Ethiopian officer go on his way rejoicing? Because he was now a Christian, a child of God; he had been saved from his past sins; he had been translated out of the kingdom of darkness into the kingdom of God's dear Son. What evidence had he that he was pardoned? He had the strongest evidence that God could give him. Jesus said: "Heaven and earth shall pass away, but my word shall never pass away." And he also said in the great commission given to the apostles: "Go ye into all the world, and preach the gospel to every creature. He that believeth and is baptized shall be saved." (Mark 16:16, 17). This man had heard the gospel, believed it, and had been baptized, so had obeyed the word of Jesus in the commission. It would be easier for heaven and earth to pass away than for the promise of Jesus, that he would be saved, to fail.

My friend, have you become a Christian by obeying the commands that the Ethiopian officer obeyed? If not, then how can you know that you are a Christian? You may be honest, sincere, and prayerful. Paul was honest and sincere, but he was not saved till he obeyed the gospel. The Ethiopian officer was deeply religious, but he was not saved till he was born of the water and the Spirit." Do no resist the Holy Spirit like the Jews did to whom Stephen spoke. They resisted the word of God that was inspired by the Holy Spirit, and in so doing they "resisted the Spirit." If you resist the word of God, there is no promise in that word for you. Do not be afraid of the criticism of men. If you obey God, he will approve you, and that is worth more than the praise of all men.

Why wait longer and live in sin? Or why try to enter into the kingdom of God in any other way than by obeying the "law of the Spirit of life in Christ Jesus," that Paul says made him "free from the law of sin and death?" You are enduring the most degrading poverty to which a soul can be subjected; God offers you wealth and riches beyond the loftiest imagination. You are covered with shame and degradation; God offers that you may share in the honor and glory which belong to angels and to his Son. You are guilty, and justly condemned to a worse penalty of suffering than any that earth can inflict; God offers pardon, full and free. You are afflicted with a disease of the soul which is a millionfold worse than any leprosy to which flesh was ever afflicted; God offers you healing that is perfect and eternal. In a word, God offers to heal, redeem, save, immortalize, fortify, crown, and make you a joint-heir with his Son to an "inheritance incorruptible, undefiled, and that fadeth not away, reserved in heaven." O the blindness and hardness of heart that will cause you to refuse to live for ever! Come, then, eat the Bread of Life, and drink the Water of Life, and live forever.

CHAPTER XI

THE RIGHT WAY

Luke wrote to Theophilus, "That thou mightest know the certainty of the things wherein thou wast instructed." (Luke 1:4). There should not, and need not, be the least doubt as to the "certainty" of that which is believed and practiced by any believer in Christ. Yet there is serious doubt and "uncertainty" in multitudes. God is not at fault, for he has made the way plain. The "uncertainty" is not due to any lack of clearness in the word of God but to the theories of men. Many ask, "How am I to know the right way when so many different ways are taught and practiced?" There can be many wrong ways but only one right way—one way to heaven. If a way can be pointed out, every word of which can be read in the Bible, and that every well-informed Protestant says is right, may we not conclude with "certainty" that it must be the right way? We desire to do that in this chapter.

Many often say, "My greatest objection to you people of the church of Christ is that you are so sure you are right and others are wrong." Well, friend, do you think you are right? If so, then you hold the same position. If you do not think you are right, then you should seek the right way and walk in it.

How may one know the "certainty" of what he believes and practices? First, every item of teaching and practice must be clearly read in the word of God. Nothing must be left untaught or practiced and nothing may be added to that which is clearly taught in the word of God. Members of the church of Christ confidently believe that they conform to the word of God in every item of teaching and practice. This is the foundation of their confidence with reference to the "certainty" of their position. A second reason is the fact that every well-informed Protestant admits that every item of teaching and practice of the churches of Christ is right. What greater "certainty" could one have than the testimony of both the Bible and all well-informed Protestants? No special effort will be made in this writing to prove by quotations from the Bible that every item we teach and practice is plainly taught in the Bible. Plain statements of what we teach and practice will be made, and then an appeal will be made to the reader to say whether it is right or wrong. This course is pursued with the confidence that every reader will agree that the teaching and practice of churches of Christ are plainly set forth in the word of God—the only infallible standard by which to measure.

1. We teach that the Bible is the inspired word of God and contains all of the will of God to man; that the Bible should be believed and that all of its commands applying to those now living should be obeyed from the heart; that "every scripture inspired of God is also profitable for teaching, for reproof, for correction, for instruction which is in righteousness: that the man of God may be complete, furnished completely unto every good work." (II Tim. 3:16, 17). Is this wrong? Every one says it is right. On the foundation of Paul's statement that the word of God "furnishes the man of God unto every good work," we confidently build. No "good work" must be left untaught and anything not taught in the word of God is not a "good work" in a religious sense. Every Protestant bears witness that this is right.

2. We teach that Jesus was born of the Virgin Mary as the only begotten Son of God; lived a sinless life; worked many miracles that prove His claim as the Son of God. We teach that His death made a full atonement for sin; that he was raised from the dead; gave the apostles the great commission to preach the gospel to every creature. We teach that in order to qualify the apostles to carry out His commission, the Holy Spirit was poured out on them to "guide them into all truth," and "bring all things to their remembrance that He had commanded them." In other words, the Holy Spirit was given to enable them to preach the gospel without error, and to perform miracles to confirm the gospel. Does any Protestant suggest for a moment that this is wrong? Certainly not, but all say it is right.

3. We teach that the gospel must be preached just as it was preached by the apostles when guided by the Holy Spirit. Both the Bible and every Protestant testify that this is right.

4. We teach that sinners must believe that Jesus is the

Christ, the Son of God—not merely give an intellectual assent but believe with the whole heart. Is this right? Again there is not a dissenting voice.

5. We teach that the sinner must repent of all his sins; that the sinner must not only be sorry for his sins, but must hate sin and turn away from it to a holy life; that his heart must be changed and purified which, in turn, will change his whole life. Here again the word of God and every Protestant affirm that the teaching of churches of Christ is right.

6. We teach that those who come to Christ in obedience must "confess with the mouth the Lord Jesus." Every Protestant denomination requires a confession of some kind in order to become a member. The churches of Christ teach that the sinner must "confess with the mouth that Jesus is the Son of God." (See Matt. 10: 32; Luke 12: 8; Acts 8: 36, 37, 38; Rom. 10: 9, 10). There is not one believer in Christ who will say this is wrong, but all say it is right.

7. We teach that Christ commanded baptism, and that His commands must be obeyed in order for us to be saved or pardoned. "Christ became the author of eternal salvation unto them that obey Him." (Heb. 5: 9). On this point both witnesses —the Bible and every Protestant—agree.

8. We teach that in order to obey the command of Christ to be baptized one must be immersed—"buried therefore with him through baptism into death;" and "raised up to walk in newness of life." (Rom. 6: 4). Does any one say it is wrong to obey the command to be baptized? Not a single well-informed Protestant will say it is wrong. True, many say baptism, though commanded by Christ, is a non-essential. Yet, almost all Protestant denominations demand what they call baptism in order to become members of their respective organizations. Is it right to be immersed? I have never heard of any one who said it is wrong to be immersed. Many say sprinkling or pouring water on believers in Christ will do. But none say it is wrong to be immersed. Once more both witnesses, the Bible and all Protestants, agree in bearing witness that the teaching of the churches of Christ is not wrong, but right.

9. We teach that when the sinner has heard the gospel; received and retained it in is heart; believed on Christ as the

Son of God with all his heart; repented of all his sins and turned away from evil thoughts, words and deeds; confessed faith in Christ as the Son of God; and has been immersed into the name of the Father, Son and the Holy Spirit; he is pardoned, saved from past sins, is a child of God, in the kingdom or church, which is the spiritual body of Christ. Has anyone ever been heard of who would deny that such a one is pardoned and saved from all past sins? Without the shadow of a doubt, both the word of God and all Protestants bear witness to the "certainty" of that which churches of Christ teach as to where and when the sinner is saved.

"But," asks one, "is there no disagreement between the teaching of the churches of Christ and Protestant denominations?" Yes, there is some disagreement. What is the point of disagreement? Others teach that the sinner is saved immediately when he believes on Christ. In other words, they teach that the sinner is saved by faith only or alone, before he fully obeys the gospel. Suppose it were possible that the sinner is saved at the point of faith, and before he obeys the gospel. Even in that case, we are still right, for we teach all the faith in Christ that any can teach. If he is saved by faith only or at the point of faith, surely he is still saved after he fully obeys the gospel. If it be contended that the sinner is saved by faith and repentance, we stress its necessity in order to be saved as strongly as it is possible for any to do. We teach and urge all the faith and repentance that any religious people teach. So, if they are right, we are still right by their own admission. There is no question in the minds of any whether the sinner is saved at the point we teach he is saved. All agree on that. The only question that can be raised is whether the sinner is saved by faith only, or by faith and repentance before he has obeyed the gospel—before he has "obeyed from the heart that form of doctrine." (Rom. 6:17, 18). No one denies or doubts the "certainty" of the fact that the sinner is saved when he has believed on Christ with the whole heart, repented of all past sins, confessed his faith in Christ and been immersed. All doubts and "uncertainty" are in regard to what others teach, but no doubts or "uncertainty" about what the churches of Christ teach.

10. All religious peoples have a form of worship that they observe when they assemble, but all do not observe the same acts of worship. No Protestant would join the Catholics in their worship when they burn incense, count beads, pray to the Virgin Mary, and such-like religious practices. The only reason offered is that the Lord did not command such things to be done as worship in the church he established. When members of the churches of Christ assemble, they engage in the "apostles' doctrine" or teaching, "in fellowship" or the contribution, "in prayers," "singing spiritual songs," and breaking bread" which is the Lord's supper. (Acts 2:41, 42; Eph. 5: 19). The church established by Christ in New Testament times observed these five acts of worship and no more. The churches of Christ today observe these five acts of worship and no more. That this is right is borne witness to by both the Bible and all Protestants. Not a single act of worship observed by the churches of Christ is in doubt. All doubts are in regard to acts of worship, observed by Protestants, that the Lord did not command.

11. The churches of Christ observe the communion or the Lord's supper every first day of the week, Sunday. All say it is right to observe the Lord's supper, but many say once a year or four times a year will do. None says it is wrong to eat of the Lord's supper every Lord's day. Again, all declare that the practice of the churches of Christ is right. Not one says it is wrong. There is not one who calls it in question.

12. Each local church of Christ, with its elders and deacons, and guided by the word of God, manages its own affairs—is independent of all outside authority. There is no conference, board of bishops, synod, convention, missionary board, or any other form of ecclesiastical organization formed by uninspired men to write creeds, make laws and govern believers in Christ by assuming the lawmaking and governing authority that belong alone to Christ as supreme king and lawgiver to rule his people. The churches of Christ in form of government, laws by which ruled—the word of God, acts of worship, names accepted, and every other particular are exact reproductions of the first model congregation formed by Christ through the work of the Holy Spirit operating through the Lord's apostles.

"Even as Moses is warned of God when he is about to make the tabernacle: for, See, saith he, that thou make all things according to the pattern showed thee in the mount." (Heb. 8:5). God showed Moses a "pattern" and commanded him to make the tabernacle—which was a type of the church—according to that "pattern." In New Testament times, He established "pattern" congregations under the direct guidance of the Holy Spirit. The churches of Christ today are the exact reproductions of those models. The churches of Christ acknowledge Christ as their king and only law-giver. Is this all wrong? No one will say it is wrong, but all unite in saying it is right. All questions of doubt are in regard to what others do in these matters. Is it right to form a denomination which in its form and its government is entirely different from that institution which the Lord formed? Is it right to ignore Christ as our only lawgiver, and allow uninspired men to write creeds, make laws and govern believers in Christ? Is it right to form an ecclesiasticism, model after that of the Roman Catholics in many particulars, even though in a modified form? The serious question of doubt is in regard to what others teach and practice. Shall Christ rule His subjects by His law—the gospel? Or, shall uninspired men legislate and make creeds and laws of their own to rule the subjects of Christ the king?

The word "church," as used in the New Testament, sometimes refers to all the saved in Christ, and sometimes to the local congregation. We refer to the saved in Christ as the church, the church of God and often as the church of Christ. These are names applied to the church as a whole or to a local congregation by the Holy Spirit as He spoke and wrote through the apostles. Again, every one says this is right; no one says it is wrong.

13. We call the individual members of the church of Christ Christians. We insist that others should call us by the name, "Christian." Yet, others persist in calling us by a nickname that we utterly reject. All other religious people are treated as they would have others treat them. They are called by the names they call themselves. But others will not treat us as they wish to be treated in the name they wear. Why is this? Should we select any title not taught by the Lord and call our-

selves by it, they would be glad to call us by that humanly formed name. Then why not just call us Christians, the name we call ourselves? Is it because we desire to wear the name of Christ only while others add another name? It is our desire that all believers in Christ should wear no other name than that of Christian. Is it right to wear no name except Christian? (See Isa. 2:2, 3; Acts 4:12; 11:26; I Peter 4:16).

The only question is whether it is right to reject the name Christian and wear some other name. Is the church the bride of Christ? (See: I Cor. 11:2; Rev. 21:2). Will the wife who loves and honors her husband wear any other name than his name? Can a wife honor her husband by adding another name to that of her husband and giving it her preference? At the very least, this is just what denominations do in regard to the religious names they wear. Ask any one of them by what name he calls himself religiously, and without an exception he will tell you he is a Methodist, a Baptist, a Presbyterian or some other religious name not mentioned in the word of God —names that the Lord never gave to the members of His church which is His spiritual bride. Do you wish to call yourself by a name the Lord never gave to His people? Is it not enough to wear His name only—just be called a Christian?

Suppose that tonight every book that has ever been written on religion except the Bible should be destroyed, and that every line on religion written or printed anywhere which is not plainly recorded in the Bible should be erased and destroyed. Suppose further, that every doctrine, practice and name not recorded in the Bible should be utterly forgotten tonight so that they never could be remembered again. Suppose that all this should happen tonight, what would be the religious condition tomorrow? There would be millions of believers in Christ who would not so much as know the religious names by which they had called themselves. They are not written in the Bible, and would have been destroyed and forgotten. Not a single denomination, from the Catholics down, could carry on its religious work and government. They would be in the utmost confusion. Their creeds by which they direct their work and worship and govern themselves would have been destroyed and forgotten. Much of their worship is not recorded in the Bible, and would be forgotten. Their creeds would be no more than blank pages except for a few disjointed, misapplied quotations from the Bible remaining. Every sentence not recorded in the Bible would have faded and left blank pages. As astounding as it may seem, not a single denomination could establish legal title to a single foot of land. The lines in their deeds where their religious names had been, and in which names they formerly held their title, would be blank, and their religious names would have been forgotten. Yes, the lines where their religious names—Methodist Church, Baptist Church, Presbyterian Church, and all others not recorded in the Bible—had been recorded would be blank, and no legal title could be established.

Destroy every book written on religion except the Bible, erase every sentence wherever found, printed or written, on religion that cannot be read in the Bible, forget every item of teaching and practice not clearly recorded in the Bible at one time, and it would not disturb churches of Christ in the least measure. Every item that is taught and practiced by churches of Christ, whether it be how to become a Christian, the kind of church government, the officers and their duties, or how to worship, can be read plainly from the Bible. Their legal title to land would be secure.

No denomination will endorse the creed, form of church government, terms of admission into the church, or the name of any other denomination. No two denominations agree on the things just mentioned. Each denomination accepts its own creed, laws, worship, government and name and rejects all others. No two denominations endorse each other. But none will affirm that any item taught and practiced by churches of Christ is wrong. The teaching and practice that can be read in every item from the word of God and which is endorsed as right by all denominations has the seal of "certainty" that it is right.

CHAPTER XII

LITTLE DUTIES

Jesus taught regardless of the circumstances in which he was situated or the number of hearers. He taught by the seaside, sitting on the mountain when a multitude was before him, to a lone woman as he sat at the well, or in the home of his friends. In the 14th chapter of Mark, we find him in the house of Simon the leper. We would think that while eating in a friend's house would not be a very good time or place to preach one of our "big" sermons. But Jesus taught a lesson much needed in our day.

A woman having a box of ointment, or perhaps as we would say, perfume, poured it on the head of Jesus. Some of those who were present indignantly said, "Why was this expensive ointment wasted? Why should it not have been sold and given to the poor?" How like we think and act today. We are often more concerned about what others do or do not do than we are about our own duties. What we should do is far more important for us to consider. Our example is often worth more than our criticism.

Jesus said, "Let her alone; why trouble ye her? She hath wrought a good work on me." The sacrifice of the ointment did not do Jesus' body any material good. It was only an expression of her love for him. He gave it his approval.

A question often comes up in regard to costly flowers at funerals. Perhaps this practice is often carried to an extreme. But Jesus most certainly commends such expressions of affection within proper limits. It is far better, however, to give some of our flowers while the loved one can see and appreciate them than to try to make up for the neglect to the one in the casket when it is too late. Visit the sick, the distressed, the broken hearted today. Speak the kind word and extend the helping hand to the weary pilgrim as he struggles with his load. Such need all the help they can get. "Bear ye one anothers burdens, so fulfill the law of Christ." The earthly house of the loved one, silent in the casket, is beyond our aid. Let us speak the kind word and do the kind deed today. There may be no tomorrow. There is no return of the neglected opportunity.

"For ye have the poor with you always, and whensoever ye will ye may do them good; but me ye have not always." We do not have Jesus with us in person as he was with those in Simon's house, but we do have him always with us in the persons of his lowly servants. When he comes on the throne of his glory to gather all the heirs of salvation, he will say to those on his right hand, "Come, ye blessed of my father, inherit the kingdom prepared for you from the foundation of the world: For I was hungry, and ye gave me to eat; I was thirsty, and ye gave me to drink; I was a stranger, and ye took me in; naked, and ye clothed me; sick, and in prison and ye came unto me." They ask, "When did we minister unto thee?" "And the king shall answer and say unto them, verily I say unto you, Inasmuch as ye did it unto one of my brethren, even the least, ye did it unto me." (Matt. 25). If Jesus were here in person today, we would be glad to show him any kindness possible. Our faith is so weak that we do not treat his "least brethren" with the same kindness with which we would treat him were he here in person. Any kindness shown to the weak children of the Lord, Jesus says, is shown to him. Any act of unkindness shown the least in the kingdom, he says, is shown to him. One of the most remarkable truths expressed in the word of the Lord is that he regards himself so closely identified with the weak, struggling children of God. This truth should make the least of us rejoice and give thanks that we are so precious to him. It should move the strongest to a serious consideration of his responsibility to serve the Lord in what he does toward the humblest Christian. It should deter us from slighting in the least measure anyone for whom Christ died. If we would stress this lesson of Jesus half as strongly as we do Mark 16:16 and Acts 2:38, we would grow more like him. We should do the one, and not leave the other undone.

Jesus said of the woman who annointed him, "She hath done what she could." The highest praise that God can give is, "You have done what you could." And every one may do that well from the greatest to the least. What we can do depends upon our ability and the need of others. If one in sorrow needs only kind words of sympathy, then kind words are all that we can give. But if more than kind words is needed—if it is in our power to give aid in material things, then kind words only will not be approved by the Lord. James says, "If a brother or sister be naked and in lack of daily food, and one of you say unto them, Go in peace, be ye warmed and filled; and yet give them not the things needful to the body; what doth it profit?" (James 2:15, 16).

I have headed this chapter with the word duty. For many years I have tried to avoid using the word duty when speaking of or writing about our service to the Lord. But I cannot find another word that makes clear the things mentioned in this chapter. Duty is an obligation that must be performed whether pleasant or unpleasant. To be acceptable, service to the Lord must be willingly and cheerfully given. The Lord used the word duty once: "Even ye also, when ye shall have done all things that are commanded you, say, We are unprofitable servants; we have done that which it was our duty to do." (Luke 17:10). It is we that are profited by our obedience, not the Lord. We say, "It is our duty to attend the worship," and we pray to the Lord to "bless all for whom it is our duty to pray." Is it our duty to breathe the air and to eat food to sustain our lives? Is it the duty of the sick to be nursed into health again? All that we receive from God is unmerited favor, and should be received with humble and thankful hearts.

Jesus said, "Verily I say unto you, Wheresoever the gospel shall be preached throughout the whole world, that also which this woman hath done shall be spoken of for a memorial of her." The act of kindness of this woman was not only praised to the people then present, but it was recorded for the encouragement of others throughout the whole world until the end of time. The humble act of love now may not be published in newspapers, or even reported in the neighborhood, but it will be entered on the record in heaven. What more could one desire than to be assured that the Lord sees and will reward his deed. The Lord praised people for their good deeds. Commendation wisely given is a powerful incentive to anyone. The desire to be approved is one of the most impelling motives in normal conduct. Only when one values the praise of men more than the praise of God will it influence him to unworthy deeds. Flattery is unmerited praise given to gain some personal advantage. Praise wisely given will do much to encourage even little children to unselfish, worthy deeds. We are often free with criticism but sparing in giving praise. To tell the preacher, sincerely, that we have been helped by his sermon will assure him that his work is appreciated and, therefore, encourage him in his efforts. It would be good also to tell our elders that we appreciate their toil in making the worship edifying and helpful. Their work, is at times, the most difficult of any assigned to men. They are often the most unjustly criticised of any servants of the Lord. We are often greatly lacking in our appreciation of these worthy servants of the Christ.

We say to ourselves, "If we could do some great thing, we would be glad to do it. What little I can do will not amount to much. It will scarcely be missed." This is a selfish view. We fail to realize that it is not what others do for us but what we do for others that gives us a measure of joy. The personal satisfaction that we have helped, even in a small measure, to lighten the burden and smooth the rough pathway of a fellow traveler is our greatest reward. Jesus said, "It is more blessed to give than to receive." How few of us have learned this lesson. The feeling that we can do so little that it will not amount to much, is the reason why the stream of good is so narrow and shallow and moves so slowly. It ought to be wide and deep and should flow swiftly. If we should give the little springs that make up the Mississippi River the power of choice and action like we have, and let them reason and act like we often do, the head spring would say, "I am so little that I do not amount to much; I will not be missed; no one praises me down at St. Louis; I will cease to flow." The result would be that great river would become a dry channel. A great number of our seemingly little and insignificant efforts unite to make the stream of good a mighty river of glory to God and service to man.

If we use our little talent, whatever it may be, for the good of others, we would probably use greater talent if we had it. But the general rule is that the more brilliant the intellect and the greater the ability to make money, the greater will be the temptation to use these gifts for selfish ends. The humblest life made up of "little services" will build a great life. The greatest lives are builded by the performances of little duties to the best of one's ability. It is by the faithful performance of little duties that strength is developed to accomplish great things as the world estimates greatness. What we may call little, unimportant acts the Lord may call great deeds. He has a different scale by which he measures deeds. On one occasion, he was in the temple and sat over near the treasury observing how the people made their gifts. "Many that were rich gave much." "And a poor widow came in and gave two mites that make a farthing." This was less than two cents. Had we been there, we would likely have reasoned in our hearts, "If I could give as much as one of those rich men, I would give it. It would amount to something. If I could not give more than two mites, it would not amount to anything, and I would be ashamed to give so little." Jesus, however, "called unto him his disciples, and said unto them, Verily I say unto you, this poor widow cast in more than they all that are casting into the treasury: for they all did cast in of their superfluity; but she of her want did cast in all that she had, even all her living." I have long thought that this statement of the Lord is one of the most encouraging to the "little ones" of all that he has said. Here is the least gift as measured by human standards that is recorded in history, but Jesus gave it the highest praise of all recorded gifts. This applies to all that we do or give whether it be kind words, the helping hand, or the giving of money.

We are so inclined to walk by sight rather than by faith. We are influenced too much by how things look to men rather than by how they look to God. His rule of measurement is different from that of men. Jesus said, "And whosoever shall give to drink unto one of these little ones a cup of cold water only, in the name of a disciple, verily I say unto you he shall in no wise lose his reward." (Matt. 10:42). An act of service may be little as we measure things, but great enough that the Lord approves and will reward.

God has one rule by which he measures greatness, and

only one. The apostles were human as we are human. Even as we, they wanted to be great, to have positions of prestige, and to rule over others. Two of them requested that they have a place—one on his right hand and the other on his left hand—in his kingdom. This ambition to have places of preeminence caused the first dissention among the apostles. Jesus said, "But he that is great among you, let him become as the younger; and he that is chief, as he that doth serve." (Luke 2:26). Again, he said, "For the Son of man came not to be ministered unto, but to minister, and give his life a ransom for many." (Matt. 20:28). The least of us can be a humble servant. Greatness in the kingdom of the Lord is measured by service. He who serves most is accounted the greatest in God's sight. What a blessing that greatness with God is within the reach of the least of us. Each can hear the welcome plaudit, "Well done thou good and faithful servant; enter thou into the joy of thy Lord."

CHAPTER XIII

GREAT DAYS

In the history of nations, there are great days that mark the dividing lines between epochs. So it is in the history of time.

The day that God made man in his own likeness was a great day. It marked the beginning of a new race. It was the day of the crowning work of creative intelligence.

The day that man yielded to the temptation of Satan was the saddest day of all time. It separated man from God, his Creator. It was the beginning of all sorrow, and of death itself. From that day has come all the sadness and suffering of a dying world. It was the beginning of sin, and from sin has come all that is evil.

The day that God gave the promise, "the seed of the woman shall bruise the serpent's head," was the first glad day after sin brought sorrow. It gave the first hope of redemption from Satan, sin, and death.

The day that Noah entered the ark was a sad day, a day of justice and judgment when a sinful, rebellious world, except eight souls, was destroyed.

The day that God called Abraham out of his native country into a strange land was a great day. It served to keep alive in an idolatrous world the worship of the one, true God. It made possible the preparation of a people to whom prophets were sent, who were made the keepers of the Oracles of God, and from whom the Redeemer came.

The day the Israelites were delivered from their bondage was a great day. It typifies a later deliverance from sin. Moses led the Israelites through the Red Sea as on dry land, then guided them through the wilderness. Through him God gave to them the law, including the ten commandments, and established a system of worship. Through the law, God prepared a people for the reception of Christ, his Anointed, and made them ready for the establishment of the kingdom of

129

heaven. It was a great day in which the star of hope was made to shine more brilliantly.

The day that Jesus was born in the stable in Bethlehem was the happiest day the world had known since sin entered. The Redeemer, announced by the holy angels, had now come. He was the first to appear on earth among men strong enough to give man victory over his enemies—Satan, sin, and death. The fulfillment of God's promise, long deferred, was at last a reality. So great was this day that the angels sang his praise and announced, "Peace on the earth, good will to men, glory to God in the highest."

The day that Jesus withstood the temptation of Satan was a great day. For the first time, it was proved that one dwelling in the flesh was strong enough to resist the Devil, and to conquer him.

The day that Jesus died on the cross was, seemingly, the greatest defeat since man sinned and fell. Yet, it was actually the greatest victory in man's behalf that had ever occurred. It was the one and only sacrifice that could take away sin. It was the blood shed in his death that alone could cleanse the soul from the stain of sin caused by man's yielding to Satan, and thus renew in man the image of God which he bore in Paradise. The death of Jesus marked the greatest day since creation.

The three days that Jesus lay in the tomb were the darkest days since creation. The long promised Redeemer had come, but Satan had secured his death. During those three days the hope of the world hung by the brittlest thread since the fall. For three days, the hope of a lost world hung on the promise expressed in three words by him who lay in the embrace of death. Jesus had said, "I will arise." Unless this promise is fulfilled, the world must forever remain without hope—eternally separated from God—lost!

The day that Jesus arose from the dead was, therefore, to that hour, the greatest day of time. He burst assunder the gates of Hades, conquered death, brought the assurance of immortality, answered the age-old question, "If a man die, shall he live again?" and gave irrefutable proof that he is able to give eternal life to all who "love his appearing."

The day that Jesus ascended to heaven and sat down at the right hand of God was a glorious day even in heaven itself. There is no other recorded announcement like unto that which was heard in heaven on the day of his coronation: "Lift up your heads, O ye gates, and be ye lifted up, ye everlasting doors; and king of glory shall come in."

The day of Pentecost was the greatest day of all past time. It was the day the Holy Spirit was bestowed upon twelve men enabling them to speak in languages they had never been taught, and "guiding them into all truth." It was the day Jesus was first proclaimed risen from the dead, the Son of God, the long looked-for Redeemer, and the crowned king at God's right hand. It was the first day that actual remission of sins had ever been offered and accepted by lost sinners. It was the day on which the "little stone was cut out without hands," that was to become a "great mountain and fill the whole earth." It was the day the kingdom was set up by the God of heaven to stand forever. It was the birthday of the church of God, in which all promised spiritual blessings were fulfilled. Measured by every standard, the day of Pentecost transcends any other day of past time.

The day of the coming of the Lord, "when he shall sit on the throne of his glory, accompanied by all the Holy angels," will be the greatest of all days. In it, time will end, the judgment will be set, and all nations will stand before him. For the impenitent and rebellious, it will be the saddest of all days. For the pure in heart, it will be the happiest day of all time. It will be the end of all sorrows and the beginning of unalloyed joy. It will be the day of final redemption from sin, and entrance into the everlasting city of God, beyond the possible reach of temptation, sorrow, and death. It will be the day when the soul will exclaim, "O death where is thy sting? O grave where is thy victory?" All real joy on earth springs from this, the greatest of the desires and hopes of the soul.

CHAPTER XIV

BOOK OF REVELATION

Perhaps there has been more controversy and speculation about the Book of Revelation than about any other part of the Bible. Books almost without number have been written in an effort to explain the scenes miraculously given to John to commit to writing. Time has proved most of what has been written to be no more than the fruits of fertile imagination.

Most books commenting on Revelation deal with the opening of the seven seals, the sounding of the trumpets, and the scenes that followed. Writers have interpreted the scenes that followed the sounding as some great calamity, especially of civil war. In like manner, they have interpreted the scenes following the pouring out of the seven vials (bowls) of the "wrath of God into the earth." (Rev. 16). Such scenes have been held to be a prophetic forecast of carnal war on the earth. They interpreted such scenes as great physical destruction on earth, and gave the war, the time, and the place when such were literally fulfilled on earth. Soon after the war between the states, I. L. Martin, who lived in Indiana, claimed that the late war fulfilled one of the scenes, and earlier wars, perhaps all such prophetic scenes. In the north, Martin's book was almost regarded as an inspired document.

In the early 1890's, B. W. Johnson published a book, in which he treated the prophetic symbols after the same manner. His book is held in rather high favor by many at present. These writers, and others, used up every great scene of destruction to fit perfectly with great wars. Since they so confidently affirmed that they had the "key" unlocking the many symbolic mysteries, we have had two world wars, greater than any set forth before. I have often wondered, if the writers of such interpretations should come back to earth, and revise their books, how they would try to make the two world wars fit with the scenes in Revelation. They used them all up years before the two greatest wars in history. The reader will now ask, "Can you interpret those happenings that John saw?"

Frankly, I cannot tell you just what they signify as related in time and place on the earth. However, I am quite sure we can get the lesson in them for us. It is my confirmed judgment that many have looked at such scenes from God's side rather than the lessons in them for us. It seems to me that there are lessons in Revelation, if rightly considered, to increase our faith, courage, and hope, as there are in the epistles of the apostles. We can only briefly sketch some of the lessons we weak Christians so need to learn.

The letters, dictated to John by the Lord himself, to the seven churches are as easily understood as Paul's epistles. They should be diligently and reverently studied by individuals and especially by the whole church. Every church from the smallest to the largest can find its picture given by the Lord and vividly portrayed. Consider the church at Ephesus. Jesus commended it for holding true to the gospel teaching. He had only one reproof of that great church. "But I have this against thee, that thou didst leave thy first love." (Rev. 2:4). I have often wondered if that is not a vivid picture of many of the churches today. We glory in our opposition to human creeds, and boast of our doctrinal purity, but our love of the Lord, fervency of devotion is low. How we need to heed his admonition, "Remember therefore whence thou art fallen, and repent and do the first works; or else I come to thee and will remove thy candlestick out of its place, except thou repent." (Rev. 2:5).

After the letters to the seven churches, which it seems are as plain and practical as the epistles of the apostles. John writes: "After these things I saw, and behold, a door was opened in heaven, and the first voice that I heard, a voice as of a trumpet speaking with me, and saying, Come up hither, and I will show thee the things which must come to pass hereafter. Straightway I was in the Spirit: and behold there was a throne set in heaven, and one sitting on the throne: and he that sat was to look upon like a jasper stone and a sardis; and there was a rainbow round about the throne, like an emerald to look upon." (Rev. 4:1-3). John was given a view of heaven, and the heavenly host, around the throne, praising and worshiping God. From here to the close of Revelation, the book is made up of symbols, figures and vivid description down to the final judgment. The theme concerns a battle between right and wrong, between Christ and Satan, till the last enemy is destroyed. While no one can tell the time or place, hence interpret correctly the great calamities, set forth in symbols, yet to read and ponder the book is as helpful to Christians as any other part of God's revelations. Let us briefly consider some of the great lessons for us. The great mistake generally made is that writers try to be too much concerned about that which belongs to God, and overlook the things that relate to us.

First of all, consider the difference between the Lord and men in regard to the future of things established. Did men ever establish an enterprise or government, and tell those taking part in such arrangements that they would have to face great difficulties? Men always predict success and pleasure for the future. From the beginning, Jesus has warned those who desire to follow him that they would not have an easy time. He told the first disciples that they would be "hated of all men" for his name's sake. He said the time would come when those who killed them "would think they were doing God's service." Whosoever loved father, mother, wife or husband more than they loved him was not worthy of him. At no time did he ever tell his hearers that to follow him would be easy and pleasant from the standpoint of earth and time. The only reward he held out for them was joy in their hope for life eternal. The Holy Spirit gave a record of how the apostles were cast into prison, beaten with many stripes and killed. Not only were the early followers of Jesus made to suffer death because of their love for him, but they warned all who should live after them that they must suffer for his sake. The Holy Spirit by Paul warned that there would come a falling away, and that the man of sin would claim the authority that belongs alone to God.

The book of Revelation is largely a symbolic picture of what the servants of Jesus would suffer down to the close of time. Just suppose, if you can, that Jesus and the apostles had told their hearers that everything would be easy and pleasant, that they would be popular with the world. Had they done so, when trial and persecution came, they could have said they had been deceived, and doubtless would have turned back to their former life. How many times did Jesus say, "Watch?" How many times were hearers told that through much tribulation they must enter the kingdom. In part, Revelation is a vivid description of the suffering of Christians throughout the Gospel dispensation. Everyone who reads with this thought in view will be greatly strengthened for the trials of pilgrims on their way to a home where the soul finds rest.

One of the great needs of our generation is a deeper reverence for God manifested in spiritual worship such as characterized the first church. We sing, read some scripture, eat of the loaf and drink of the cup, but there is a great lack of humility and deep feeling. The careful reading and meditation on what John saw in his vision will create in our hearts a greater spirit of worship than we have ever experienced.

He saw around the throne of God twenty-four thrones. On them sat twenty-four elders. These were seven lamps of fire burning before the throne which are the seven spirits of God. Before the throne there was as it were a sea of glass, clear as crystal. Around about the throne he saw four living creatures (not beasts as the King James gives it). Each of these had six wings, and was full of eyes. "And they have no rest day and night, saying: Holy, holy, holy, is the Lord God, Almighty, who was and who is and who is to come." The four and twenty elders fall down and worship him, saying: "Worthy art thou, our Lord and our God, to receive the glory and the honor and the power; for thou didst create all things, and because of thy will they are, and were created." (Rev. 4:4-11). Our aim and hope is to attain to the presence of God and worship him. Our worship here and now is to train and prepare us to worship God in his immediate presence. With what reverence and humility should we strive to present ourselves before him here below.

The record in the fifth chapter says that John saw in the hand of God who sat on the throne a book written on the inside and outside, with seven seals. Search was made in heaven and earth for a man to open the seals. At first, no one was found able to open the seals. This caused John to weep much. One of the elders told him not to weep; that the "Lion of the tribe of Judah, the Root of David, hath overcome to open the book and the seven seals thereof." It is very plain that this was Christ himself. The book contained a prophetic, symbolic picture. The scenes described under the opening of each of the six seals, and the voice of seven thunders picture, in imagery, time until the judgment, and the glories of the home of the redeemed.

When the first seal was opened, there was heard as it were a "Voice of thunder, Come and see." John saw four horses on which were four riders. I shall ask the reader to bear with me while I express my opinion as to the meaning of the scene. It is an opinion that I have never stated in a sermon or in writing. Opinions are harmful when they are persistently stressed and pressed to the disturbance of peace.

The first horse was white. The rider had a bow but no arrow. A crown was on his head, and "he went forth conquering, and to conquer." It is my opinion that this symbolizes Christ, marching through time, after he was crowned King in heaven till he has conquered the last enemy. In Revelation 19: 11, John tells what he saw again. "And I saw the heaven opened; and behold, a white horse, and he that sat thereon called Faithful and True; and in righteousness he doth judge and make war." This removes all doubt that the first horseman was Christ himself.

When the second seal was opened, he saw a "red horse and to him that sat thereon it was given to take peace from the earth, and that they should slay one another; and there was given him a great sword." To me, this rider symbolizes carnal war. Wherever there is carnal war, there the red horse and his rider are on the march.

When the third seal was opened, he saw a black horse on which sat a man. The rider had a balance in his hand. The price of wheat and barley was given, extremely high in price. Scarcity of food follows wars. It has been estimated that more people die for lack of food than are killed in battle. This is true in countries ravaged by war. We in America have not been ravaged by war by the invasion of a foreign army.

When the fourth seal was opened, another horseman appears. "And I saw, and behold, a pale horse; and he that sat upon him, his name was Death; and Hades followed with him. And there was given unto them authority over the fourth part of the earth, to kill with the sword, and with famine, and with death, and by the wild beasts of the earth." (Rev. 6). Many have tried to show that these events happened in the past, and have located the time and place when and where they were fulfilled in past wars. But, two world wars have come since, and their wars of the past had been used up. This is the difficulty they find themselves in who try to fit the great vision in Revelation to dates in time and past wars. It is our opinion, as previously stated, that the four horses represent happenings repeated often during time until Jesus comes for the faithful.

When the fifth seal was opened, John saw "underneath the altar the souls of them that had been slain for the word of God and the testimony which they held" pleading to know how long till God would "judge and avenge our blood on them that dwell on the earth?" To each was given a white robe. They were told to "rest for a little while, till others who suffer like martyrdom should be killed." When this vision shall be fulfilled, as it is yet in the future, I do not have an opinion. The lesson for me is: (1) those who are faithful to the Lord will surely be richly rewarded; and (2) the wicked may rule for a while, but God will surely bring them to judgment. This lesson gives strength to the servants of the Lord that will sustain them in' the greatest trial and suffering, and it is a solemn warning to the wicked that they will not go unpunished.

The opening of the sixth seal revealed an earthquake so great that the light of the sun was blotted out; the moon became as blood; the stars of heaven fell to the earth like ripe figs falling when the tree is shaken by a great wind. "And the heaven removed as a scroll when it is rolled up; and every mountain and island were moved out of their places." Kings and the great and small of men hid themselves in the caves and rocks of the mountains and called on them to, "Fall on us, and hide us from the face of him that sitteth on the throne, and from the wrath of the Lamb; for the great day of their wrath is come; and who shall be able to stand?"

When and in what manner these awful punishments will

come on earth, no one but God knows. But we know that it will be visited upon the willfully disobedient. The lesson for us is that we should faithfully serve the Lord. The worst that can come upon the faithful is the death of the house in which we now live. That must cone to all whether good or evil. Only the second death need to be feared by Christians. Let us be concerned about our side—faithfulness in His service. It is a warning to the wicked and an exhortation to the righteous.

The seventh chapter records the sealing of 144,000. Who were they? The angel told John, "These are they that came out of great tribulation and they washed their robes and made them white in the blood of the Lamb." More than this, we are not told. But is that not enough?

No one can read and meditate on the fearful things signified by the symbols from the eighth to and including the nineteenth chapter without being overwhelmed with Godly fear, and impressed with the need of humbly serving God.

This brings us to the twentieth chapter. More has been written, perhaps, about this chapter than any other part of the Bible. It would be profitless, even if space permitted, to name the theories formulated hundreds of years ago, down even till this day. Many in the denominational churches are putting out conflicting, fantastic speculations on the chapter. Let us consider briefly some theories advanced by our own brethren. Some say that the 1,000 years began when the Gospel was first preached on Pentecost. They say the chain with which Satan was bound is the chain of evidence. They say that the 1,000 years is an indefinite period of time and will continue till Christ returns at the end of time. If that is true, then why stress it? How to become Christians and how to serve is easily undersood. When the 1,000 years began, or begins, belong to God, not to us.

Others affirm that the 1,000 years is in the future. They say that, when the period is ushered in, Christ will set up his kingdom on earth, and reign a literal 1,000 years. Much strife and disturbance has been caused by persistently stressing this theory. Now just suppose that this theory turns out to be right. In that case, it cannot have any bearing on our lives now. We certainly are not living in such a future period. Again, that is God's side, not ours. What, then, are the lessons for us? Is there anything to give us strength? Most assuredly there is a great lesson that the humblest of us can understand.

"And I saw an angel coming down out of heaven, having the key of the abyss and a great chain in his hand. And laid hold on the dragon, the old serpent, which is the Devil and Satan, and bound him for a thousand years, and cast him into the abyss, and shut it, and sealed it over him, that he should deceive the nations no more, until the thousand years should be finished; after this he must be loosed a little time." Is it not good to know that the Lord, whom we so imperfectly serve, is able to bind Satan for a time called a thousand years? Greater is he that is for us than he that is against us. Why should we worry, argue and cause confusion when the thousand years will be, and whether it is just a thousand years as we record time, or a period of much greater length? All that belongs alone to God. It is ours to faithfully serve him, and leave to him all matters that are not within our power to perform.

"And I saw thrones, and they sat upon them, and judgment was given unto them." Where were these thrones? Who sat on them? It could be the apostles.

"And Jesus said unto them, Verily I say unto you, that ye who have followed me, in the regeneration when the Son of man shall sit on the throne of his glory, ye also shall sit upon twelve thrones, judging the twelve tribes of Israel." (Matt. 19:28). But again, that belongs to the Lord. John also "saw the souls of them that had been beheaded for the testimony of Jesus, and for the word of God, and such as worshiped not the beast, neither his image, and received not the mark upon their foreheads and upon their hand; and they lived and reigned with Christ a thousand years." (Rev. 20:1-4). Jesus said, "And I say unto you my friends, Be not afraid of them that kill the body, and after that have no more that they can do. But I will warn you whom ye shall fear; Fear him, who after he hath killed hath power to cast into hell; yea, I say unto you, Fear him." (Luke 12:4-5). There is no known power that can cause the Christian to lose his reward except his own surrender to Satan. The martyr wins a glorious victory.

After sketching this far through the Bible, we come to the

record of what John saw—the judgment of all mankind, beginning with Adam and ending with the last to live and die on the earth. It is a gathering to which all will come from the least to the greatest. The humblest servant and the greatest rulers of all time will be there. Yes, dear reader, you and I will stand before the Judge of all men. No such scene has ever been visualized by the most fertile imagination. "And I saw a great white throne, and him that sat upon it, from whose face the earth and heaven fled away; and there was found no place for them. And I saw the dead, the great and the small, standing before the throne; and another book was opened, which is the book of life; and the dead were judged out of those things which were written in the books, according to their works. And the sea gave up the dead that were in it; and death and Hades gave up the dead that were in them; and they were judged every man according to their works. And death and Hades were cast into the lake of fire. This is the second death, even the lake of fire. And if any was not written in the book of life, he was cast into the lake of fire." (Rev. 20:11-15). This is the picture painted by the Holy Spirit of the assembly in which each of us must be present. This meeting that awaits every one fills us with the most solemn reflections. It marks the end of time and the morning of eternity. The door of mercy is forever closed to those who have refused God's offer of mercy. That the wicked must be turned away is the most terrible thought which can engage the mind. If the wicked could be permitted to enter into the presence of God, it could not make them happy. They have no love for holy association.

God's mercy is great, and it will take all his mercy to admit the best of us into heaven. When I try to measure myself by the sermon on the mount, and see how far I am below that teaching, I am made humble and impressed with my unworthiness. Let us try to be able to hear, "Well done, enter thou into the joy of the Lord."

One may become rich in material things, attain fame and be counted a great success, but if his name is not written in the Lamb's book, he has failed for eternity. One may be poor in the goods of this world, endure hardships and be held in low esteem by the world; yet, if his name is found written in the Lamb's book of life, he has an inheritance incorruptible and as enduring as eternity.

The 21st and 22nd chapters of Revelation give the most joyous view of the glories and blessings that God has prepared for the redeemed. The Holy Spirit has portrayed the riches of heaven. "And I saw a new heaven and a new earth: for the first heaven and the first earth are passed away; and the sea is no more. And I saw the holy city, new Jerusalem, coming down out of heaven from God, made ready as a bride adorned for her husband. And I heard a great voice out of the throne saying, Behold, the tabernacle of God is with men, and he shall dwell with them, and they shall be his people, and God himself shall be with them. And be their God; and he shall wipe every tear from their eyes; and death shall be no more; neither shall there be mourning, nor crying, nor pains, any more; the first things are passed away." (Rev. 21:1-b).

It would be irreverent, I think, to try to comment on the last two chapters of God's revelation to man. Read the chapters, and meditate upon the glorious blessings awaiting us if we are faithful till we are called to our inheritance.

"And God said, Behold, the man has become as one of us, to know good and evil; and how, lest he put forth his hand, and take of the tree of life, and eat, and live forever: therefore Jehovah God sent him forth from the garden of Eden." (Gen. 3:22-23). Preventing man from eating of the tree of life and so becoming immortal in sin, was God's first act of mercy to fallen man.

"Blessed are they that do his commandments, that they may have right to the tree of life, and enter in through the gates into the city." (Rev. 22:14).

Printed in the United States
20634LVS00001B/409-429

9 781584 270768